IVAN
Ramen

IVAN
Ramen

Love, Obsession, and
Recipes from Tokyo's Most
Unlikely Noodle Joint

Ivan Orkin

with Chris Ying

TEN SPEED PRESS
Berkeley

All rights reserved.
Published in the United States by Ten Speed Press, an imprint of the
Crown Publishing Group, a division of Random House, Inc., New York.
www.crownpublishing.com
www.tenspeed.com

Ten Speed Press and the Ten Speed Press colophon are registered
trademarks of Random House, Inc.

Photographs on front cover and pages vi, xii, 2, 50, 88 to 89, 90, 109,
121, 133, 134, 136, 141, 142, 144, 148, 149, 150, 153, 154, 159, 172, 182, 187,
188, 196, and 204 by Daniel Krieger, copyright © 2013 by Daniel Krieger

Photographs on back cover and pages viii, 14, 17, 19, 30, 36, 38, 39, 40, 43,
47, 48 to 49, 55, 56, 57, 59, 62, 64, 66 to 67, 68, 70, 74, 78, 80 to 81, 83,
84, 93, 95, 98, 101, 102, 106, 110, 112, 118, 122, 125, 126, 130, 129, 160, 168,
175, 176, 192, and 195 by Noriko Yamaguchi

Photographs on pages 4, 7, 8 to 9, 12, 24 to 25 (top left, top right, and
bottom left), 28, 33, 60, and 77 from Ivan Orkin

Photographs on pages 22 and 25 (bottom) by Sharp Images Photographic,
www.sharpimagesphotographic.com

Photograph on page 201 by Chris Ying

Library of Congress Cataloging-in-Publication Data is on file with
the Publisher

Hardcover ISBN: 978-1-60774-446-7
eBook ISBN: 978-1-60774-447-4

Printed in China

Design by Chris Ying and Walter Green
Production by Sarah Adelman
Illustrations by Walter Green

10 9 8 7 6 5 4 3 2 1

First Edition

This book is dedicated to my father, Leonard Orkin, who died suddenly on February 1, 2013, shortly before its completion. He was the source of so much inspiration, and my inability to share this book with him leaves me deeply saddened. His presence is in these pages and in my heart. Like any great father, he prepared me for all the challenges I've met over the years. My success is his. Although at times it must have seemed that I heard not a word he said to me, I was always listening very carefully. Thanks, Dad. This book's for you.

Contents

Foreword

Hey Ivan!

First off, congratulations on—and thank you for—this book. Back when I was a twenty-nothing noodle-slurping lost sheep wandering from ramen shop to ramen shop, trying to decode the secrets of the soup, there was nothing like this in English, or maybe in any language. There is so much essential, indispensible information here for readers who want to learn something about ramen beyond the instructions on the side of the Styrofoam bowl. And then there's your story, which is beyond remarkable: I couldn't get a job in a decent shop when I was in Japan. You've broken through the ramen barrier in Tokyo, put your name on the map. Incredible.

And now you're going to open a shop in New York! Well, let me be the first to congratulate you on a terrible decision. Here's the best advice I can give you about trying it back home:

1. Do you know the classic 1992 Wesley Snipes—Woody Harrelson buddy basketball movie *White Men Can't Jump*? Of course you do! What you might not know is that your next year is going to be an infinite loop of a sad variation of that film: *White Men Can't Eat Ramen.*

When you put a hot bowl of ramen in front of most Americans—white or otherwise—they will wait for it to cool down. It defeats the purpose, but they do not know this. It's the equivalent of ordering a burger, and then when it comes, you don't touch it! You wait for it to cool down, the lettuce to wilt, the cheese to congeal.

Americans think it's rude to slurp noodles. They have no concept that the noodles are continuing to cook in the soup. They have no concept that they should drink the soup first. And they will think the soup is too salty! They don't understand that the soup is part of the noodles.

I know this. I've seen thousands and thousands of bowls at Momofuku. People have been leaving behind noodles before it was cool to be gluten free.

These will be your customers!

2. Prepare to compromise.

I've been to ramen shops in Tokyo. It'd be nice to serve sixty people a day in a twenty-seat restaurant, two bowls at a time. You won't be able to do it like that here. The economics of New York are different.

While you can sell ramen relatively expensively in Japan, you can't do it in America. People will unblinkingly pay $20 a plate for spaghetti pomodoro—which is just canned tomatoes and boxed pasta—but they will bitch to the high heavens about forking over $20 for a bowl of soup that requires three or four or five different cooked and composed components to put together. Plus, you will rake yourself over the coals looking for ingredients that even approximate what you can buy down the alley from your shop in Tokyo.

You'll have to find a way to make food faster, and that means doing some things that may be sacrilegious in Japan. You've gotta make the compromise between having the soup hot, but not so hot that people can't eat it. If you serve dishes with ramen, it's going to slow the experience down. People will have a conversation instead of eating. That's the main difference. In Tokyo, if you go to a really good ramen-ya, you hear nothing but slurping. In New York, people want to chat over their soup! It is unthinkable to those of us who have prayed at the altars of the ramen gods, but it is a reality you must confront.

3. Get ready for the most ridiculous complaints ever known to mankind.

You should shave your head now so that you have no hair to pull out when the Internet gets revving on you.

Get ready for criticism from the whole Asian demographic. Half the food bloggers in the world are Asian women. You're going to be their bread and butter. They're going to laugh at you and yell at you. They will be upset that your food isn't "authentic" or that it's not Japanese enough.

White people will say, "I've lived in Japan, and this isn't authentic." You're never going to have seen so many people express their feelings. Everybody is going to have their opinion on what Japan is. They may not have been to Japan, but you know what? They might have dated somebody from Japan.

People are going to look at you like this weird thing, like the Eminem of ramen. I can almost get away with doing ramen because I'm Asian. You're probably fucked.

Fifty percent of people will be cheering for you, and the other 50 percent will want you dead. Get ready to accept that people hate you and want nothing but your demise. Use it as fuel.

4. It's like in Band of Brothers when the guy says, "The only hope you have is to accept the fact that you're already dead."

When I opened up, people in New York didn't know anything about ramen at all. The funny thing is, people know even less about ramen today. New York is so far behind the world of contemporary ramen in Japan—a world I can't quite fathom how you conquered or why you're leaving.

What I originally loved about ramen shops in Japan was that it was a whole fascinating world. I can eat something really delicious for ten or fifteen bucks. It's exactly like going to In-N-Out and knowing the secret menu. Once you're in the know, everything's good. You know what to order.

What drew me to cooking ramen was—and I hate to use this term—the punk aesthetic. It was a contrarian stance. You take something deemed by the world as junk food and pour passion into it, and make it the most delicious food possible. In that conflict is what I love about ramen. At the end of the day, it's just soup and noodles. It's one of the simplest forms of food, but also the most beloved. And of course you know that. You're making Jewish comfort food through a Japanese lens.

And down there on the Lower East Side, where Jewish chicken soup has roots more than a century old, you will slowly build an audience that understands your soup.

Americans will fail you more times than you can anticipate, but if you're smart and steeled and shrewd—or maybe just incredibly fucking lucky—you will get what you're looking for: your customers.

There will be babies born and nourished on your food. One day they'll be nine years old, and it'll be really weird: they will have formed memories in your restaurant, on your ramen. They will learn to eat the way you want them to. You will learn from them.

You're feeding people, you're going to bring people a lot of joy. It's a heavy-duty thing when you get past all the bullshit. But do not underestimate the bullshit.

Congratulations!

–DAVID CHANG

PS: Once you open the restaurant, all of the emails you will ever get will look like this: *Can I have a reservation for 6 people at the ramen counter at 8:30 tonight? I know it's Saturday and you just got reviewed but I'm coming in with this great group of . . .*

Prologue

I'm sitting at the counter of what used to be Ed's Lobster Bar Annex, on Clinton Street in the Lower East Side. All the stools but mine are upside down on the bar. The chalkboard on the wall advertises coconut shrimp and lobster fra diavolo as the day's specials.

The restaurant has been closed for a few months, but it still looks like it's just waiting for someone to walk in, flick on the lights, and open the doors. Except no one will, because the keys are in my pocket. With any luck, in four months this will be Ivan Ramen New York.

There's nothing notable about someone opening a restaurant in New York. God knows how many people do it every year. These days, it's not even particularly newsworthy for someone to open a ramen shop in New York. But I didn't just show up with a folder of recipes and a pocket full of dreams. I took a more circuitous route.

In 1987, I was a disorganized, confused twenty-something. I wasn't a student. I wasn't a chef. I wasn't really anything. I had a degree in the impractical subject of Japanese literature, but I'd never even left the country. For no reason other than it seemed like the right thing to do, I bought a ticket to Japan. I ended up spending thirteen of the next twenty-five years there, as a slacker, a teacher, a computer component salesman, a husband, a widower, a father, and a chef. I opened a ramen shop in Tokyo, and then another. Eventually, a lot of people started coming to the restaurants, critics began heaping praise on my food, and journalists followed me around with cameras and microphones and questions. Me, a Jewish guy from Long Island with no prior ramen experience to speak of.

It has always struck me as somewhat odd to read a book that a chef has written about himself. But, for some reason, chefs have captured the American imagination. There's something mystical in the way they create something new out of the mundane. And maybe that's the appeal of my story. A screw-up white kid from New York, nothing about him screaming BORN FOR GREATNESS, succeeds wildly as a chef in Tokyo.

When I put it like that, it doesn't even seem real to me. It's a fairy tale, and my selfish reason for writing this book is that I want to see my fairy tale printed, bound, and displayed on a shelf. Cookbooks are special to me, and I love peering into chef's lives, sharing in their triumphs and failures and learning about their cuisines. But when I tried to learn more about

my own world—the idiosyncratic, obsessive, delicious world of Japanese ramen—I didn't find much. I've told my story thousands of times in Japan. People write me letters, saying they want to start their own shop, asking for advice. I'm always happy to share. But this book will be the first opportunity I've had to address my compatriots—my fellow Americans!

I'm a chef. I don't really open a cookbook to cook from it, and I don't know if many people do. I read cookbooks because I want to know why someone cooks the way they do, how they arrived at their recipes. It doesn't matter if the recipe is complex—molecular, whatever—or a simple one. It could be a pancake recipe, but I want to know why the author's excited about it. This book will teach you how to make an authentic bowl of Tokyo ramen, but I also encourage you to stray as much as you want from the recipes. This book is not intended to be a set of rules, but rather a window into a world I tumbled into years ago and have happily dwelled in ever since.

Whenever I set out to make a bowl of ramen in my kitchen at home, cooking every single component—stock, dashi, noodles, pork, tare (the seasoning component), eggs—is still a bit daunting, even though I've gone through the process many times now, before and since moving back to New York to open up this new shop. It's a good process—exciting, gratifying, as rewarding to make as it is to eat. You'll appreciate it, but only once you've survived it.

The same, I think, applies to life. The story in this book documents a long process—a twenty-year journey. I've been through a tremendous amount of shit. We all encounter obstacles that seem insurmountable at the time, but we often grow into better people for it. I didn't know how much I'd love Japan until I moved there. I didn't find my calling until I became a cook. And I didn't become a man until my first wife died.

Through the years, I've stepped out of my comfort zone again and again—I'm still doing it, actually—and I've never regretted it. There's quite a bit to do and quite a bit to learn, if you just take a few chances. As I set out to try and open my first restaurant in America, I've found guidance in other people's stories and cookbooks, and I want to provide some of the same. So for all the wayward youth, dissatisfied salespeople, travelers, cooks, entrepreneurs, and anybody who's ever wondered, "What if I just . . . ?" this book is for you.

Beginnings

I was fifteen years old when Dean Grabsky called me to say he'd just gotten a job at a Japanese restaurant near the local train station. The place was called Tsubo, and there was another shift open, and would I be interested in making five bucks an hour–off the books–washing dishes?

That was a lot of money for someone my age in 1978, and so it was that three days a week I found myself after school standing before huge piles of dirty dishes—dishes for soy sauce, dishes for pickles, bento boxes, rice bowls, soup bowls, bowls with the tiniest compartments I'd ever seen. No matter how hard I worked, I could never seem to make a dent in that pile. To add insult to injury, the bitchy woman from Osaka who ran the restaurant hated me and the other Americans working for her.

The job should have sucked. The only reason it didn't was the chefs— an unfailingly friendly group of Japanese guys in their twenties and thirties. They took me under their wing immediately, without question. I would come to the restaurant directly from school, dizzy with teenage hunger. On one of my first days on the job, one of the cooks noticed my plight. He cracked a raw egg and whipped it with some soy sauce, poured it over a bowl of hot rice, sprinkled some aonori (powdered seaweed) on top, and thrust it into my hands. "Here, Ivan-san," he said. "Eat this."

That dish—a dish I've had hundreds of times since and came to know as tamago kake gohan—made an immense impression on me. The hot rice steamed the egg ever so slightly, and the first slimy-creamy bite, salty like the ocean, was a bit challenging. But by the end of my first bowl, I was hooked. More importantly, I was "in" with the cooks. From then on, the staff fed me whatever they were eating: raw liver smeared in garlic, shiokara (raw squid in its own fermented guts), miso soup, the whole lineup of raw fish.

When the owner declared that feeding the dishwashers was a waste of money, the cooks brushed it off, told us not to worry, and kept cooking for us. They took care of us at every turn. One of the great memories of my youth is the time the cooks took me and Dean to the city on a Saturday to watch kung-fu movies and drink beer at their friend's restaurant.

Meeting these salt-of-the-earth Japanese guys who bent over backward to take care of us was an unexpected and revelatory turning point for me. I'd always loved food, but Japanese became my favorite. By the time I was seventeen, when we'd go out for sushi and my mom and dad would order platters, I'd say snottily, "I don't eat that way. I order by the piece."

Tsubo's insufferable owner eventually became too much for me to endure, but the seeds of a lifelong love affair with Japanese culture had been planted in that year of washing dishes there.

I grew up in a neighborhood carved out of what used to be one gigantic estate. There was the main mansion at the top of the lane, and then ten houses lining the main road. Our house was located where the pool and cabanas had once been.

Syosset is a large suburb about forty minutes from Manhattan. My family moved there when I was five years old. We lived off the beaten path, five miles from my elementary school. (NB: My mother recently revealed to me that we actually lived in the unincorporated village of Oyster Bay Cove, not Syosset. She insists that I get my facts straight, but after forty-nine years of telling people that I'm from Syosset, I'm sticking with it.)

At home, my mom was an indifferent cook. Her meatloaf was okay, but most of her dishes were things like baked chicken breasts smothered in Campbell's mushroom soup. She would have been perfectly happy to take a pill that would allow her to forego eating altogether. My dad had a few specialties—spaghetti and meatballs, paella—but in general food wasn't at the top of my family's priorities. We'd go out to eat in Manhattan now and then, but I was a pain-in-the-ass kid, so our excursions often ended early with some kind of incident involving me pestering my two sisters.

In spite of my family's culinary apathy, I developed a psychological connection with food. It wasn't based on any refined opinion about which foods were more delicious than others, but simply an association between food and warmth and love. I had a pretty lonely upbringing, and didn't really have any like-minded friends until high school. Somehow, the vision of sharing a meal with friends and family—the act of coming together to eat—became my picture of happiness.

By the end of high school, I knew in my heart that I was meant to be a cook. But in 1981 nice Jewish boys continued on the path to college; they didn't take the blue-collar road of cooking. I was a terrible student, though—a hyper, intense kid. I was kicked out of Hebrew school when I tore out the holiest prayer in the union prayer book, folded it into a paper airplane, and threw it at the teacher (with great accuracy, unfortunately). I ended up going to the only college I could get into: the University of Bridgeport, which had some kind of remedial program for delinquents like

me. Six months there, followed by a year-long stint at community college, eventually landed me at the University of Colorado.

I figured that college might be my only opportunity to live somewhere beautiful and natural, but I really chose Colorado because Boulder was one of the few schools in 1983 that offered a Japanese language program. I still had this nagging curiosity about Japanese culture, which had grown since I'd left the dishwasher job at Tsubo. I knew zero Japanese, and I don't have any sort of natural gift with languages. I'm a learn-by-doing guy, and it would take years of living in Japan, meeting Japanese people, absorbing one phrase at a time, for me to eventually get it.

Still, I insisted on majoring in Japanese. The course was built around classes in language, culture, literature, history, and poetry. I read a lot of Junichiro Tanizaki and Ogai Mori. We studied Meiji-era writers and then some contemporary ones, like Kenzaburo Oe. I was still a total shit student, but I really enjoyed Japanese literature—to this day I can hold my own in a discussion on the importance of the wayward monk in Yukio Mishima's *The Temple of the Golden Pavilion*. But mostly I got help from friends like Eric Jacobsen, who would come over in the morning and do my homework in exchange for breakfast. Eric's now a children's-television star in Tokyo.

Two weeks after graduating from Boulder, I packed up and left for Asia. On the surface, it seemed like a pretty impulsive and risky decision. Even after majoring

Top left: Hiking in the Flatirons near Boulder, with a few Japanese expats who I hung out with in college. The guy in the blue shirt was from Osaka and fed me my first mochi cakes, heated in a toaster oven. Top right: A young me, the last time I had long hair. I cut my hair right after this picture was taken, and cried as the locks fell to the floor. Bottom left: Eric Jacobsen in Tokyo. Bottom right: Another one of my infrequent camping trips as a college student in Boulder. Note the macho mustache.

in Japanese, I was by no means fluent. I had never been outside of the country.

But I'm a very practical person, and I just don't think it makes any sense to study Japanese for four years and then not immediately move to Japan. Even if my vision of modern-day Japan was a twisted, fetishized one informed by monster movies and what my dad told me about people he met at Restaurant Nippon in New York, I knew I had to go. Most people pay tens of thousands of dollars to go to school and then graduate with no ideas about what to do next. As impractical as studying Japanese might have been, at least it made the next step as clear as day. In fact, I think nearly everyone in my program went to Japan straight out of school. More than half the group headed for Osaka, but I'm a New York kid, so I decided to make my way to Tokyo. Eric had graduated the year before, and he offered to let me crash at his apartment on the outskirts of the city. My dad gave me a couple grand as a graduation present, and I was on my way.

My first stop was Taipei, where a few of my friends from the Chinese department were already living. I figured I'd get a taste for Taiwan before heading to Japan. From the moment the plane touched down, it was chaos. I disembarked the plane in a surge of Chinese people stepping all over each other. Everywhere I walked there was some steamy nastiness going on. I went to line up for the bus and my friend said, "You don't line up in Taipei," as he elbowed some old lady in the head and hip-checked another guy. In the city, the air was heavy with the smell of stinky tofu and vinegared fish. Walking the streets felt like wading. Taiwan's different now, but in 1987 it was by far the dirtiest, craziest, most aggressive place I had ever been. Granted, I'd only ever been to New York and Colorado, but that just made the culture shock all the more intense.

All we did for three weeks was eat. We'd go to a dumpling house and order massive platters of crisp, chewy, juice-filled meat bombs. We'd drink bottle after bottle of beer and eat thirty dumplings each before rolling-stumbling out of there. In the mornings, we would buy rice cakes filled with meat and drink warm soy milk. It was in Taiwan that I came to understand something fundamental about dining. It's something that people experience when they eat at David Chang's bustling restaurants or somewhere like L'Atelier de Joël Robuchon and think, "God, those chefs are geniuses." They are legitimately brilliant, and their restaurants are wonderful, but they're building on millennia of experience. The way they've integrated casual dining with high technique is something that's been happening forever in Asia.

In Asia, eating and drinking is a seamless part of living. For a long time, dining in the West—at least in many of the restaurants where I worked or ate—has seemed almost robotic by contrast. We get our food and we look down at our plates and we eat and we don't talk. When the plates are cleared, you look up for a second, and start speaking, but then the next course arrives, and everyone quiets down again. That's just not how people eat in Asia. Eating is a shared experience—hands reach across tables, utensils clank against plates and bowls, people laugh and talk and share. Going out to dinner isn't as much of an event; it's just a natural continuation of the day, part of living well.

I have Taipei and all its entropic mayhem to thank for confirming that there is indeed something special about eating with friends. But I didn't really fall in love with Asia until I landed in Tokyo. It was my first visit, but as my plane touched down at Narita International, I felt that I was coming home. Where Taipei had been anarchic and confusing, Tokyo was carefully organized. Nobody pushed, everybody quietly lined up, and people cleaned the gum off the stairs and polished the banisters at the train stations. I didn't know any of that yet, but even as I got off the plane, I could have kissed the ground in happiness.

First Encounters

I'd come to Japan at the peak of the country's economic power. The Japanese were buying Rockefeller Center and famous golf courses; it was the place to be if you were young and ambitious. Of course, that didn't really have anything to do with me. I was there because I'd majored in Japanese and I had a friend in Tokyo who'd offered to let me stay with him.

Eric was in Kunitachi, a suburb about forty minutes west of downtown Tokyo. It's a famous university town, pretty hip and funky, with a lot of wealthy residents. The house he lived in was a hundred years old, with sliding doors that opened onto a pretty little garden. But there was no running water, and the toilet was an indoor outhouse—essentially just a hole in the ground in the middle of the house with a septic system designed to accommodate one person, not two.

I didn't want to overstay my welcome, and I've always been a pretty serious job-hunter, so within my first month of being in Japan I'd found a

Left: I got talked into purchasing a motorcycle soon after arriving in Japan. I never really loved riding it, and when it was stolen three weeks after the purchase—the only act of theft I've ever experienced in Japan—I stopped riding motorcycles forever.

position teaching English at a school that would sponsor a work visa. In the eighties, Berlitz schools were the only place for Japanese people to study English. I worked at the branch in Shibuya, one of the hipper sections of Tokyo. That meant I had a steady stream of famous students, including Nobuko Miyamoto—the star of the seminal ramen film *Tampopo*— and her two kids.

In those early months, even walking into a restaurant was intimidating. With my lack of language skills, I didn't know how to order. I ate at a lot of teishoku shops, which are basically the Japanese equivalent of American diners. Back in the eighties, teishoku were everywhere—mostly independently run, each with its own unique character, much like diners in the New York and New Jersey area. (Now they've mostly disappeared and been replaced by "famires"—"family restaurants" like Denny's.) You'd get a meal of soup, some pickles, and one of ten or fifteen entrées—a piece of grilled fish or a pork-ginger sauté or some other Japanese comfort food. Like an American diner, there's comfort in the familiarity, the ritual. There's even a ritual to the way you eat your meal: you take a

bite of fish, then a little pickle, a slurp of soup, and finally a mouthful of steaming rice. Repeat. But a big part of the appeal was the fact that it was easy for a language-challenged person like me to order. It can be really tempting to just go into the same place you went yesterday, where they have pictures of the food and you can just point at what you want.

Most days, Eric had his own thing going on, and he didn't have time to coddle me. His Japanese was much better than mine, so he was enjoying life at a higher level. I would hang out with him and his friends and just have no idea what the hell they were talking about. I didn't have a girlfriend or even a group of friends I could go drinking with. But I also refused to be one of the guys that would only speak English and eat at McDonald's. I was in Japan to speak Japanese. That sounds obvious, but all around me there were foreigners living in Japan who weren't that interested in Japan. They had their English-teaching gig and the job paid well; they would teach English, go out with their American buds, get hammered, and pick up Japanese girls—that was their lifestyle.

Coming to a foreign country to set up an outpost of your own culture just struck me as disrespectful. I wasn't the sort of intense weirdo who would say, "Gomen, nihongo shika hanasenai" ("No, sorry, I only speak Japanese") if a group of English speakers asked me to go grab a beer, but I was constantly amazed that people would come all the way to this country and ignore all the amazing things around us. I met people who had been in Tokyo for seventeen years who didn't speak any Japanese. I'd look at them and think, "Are you *okay*? What's your problem? You came to live in Tokyo, but don't understand the language, don't like Japanese food, and don't feel like trying to fix either situation. You've created a bizarre little English-speaking world in downtown Tokyo." One guy I met had a wife who didn't speak any English, and even their two kids didn't speak English very well either—he couldn't talk to his own kids! He wasn't a bad guy, but what a tragic life.

The travelers who have successful experiences are the people who are willing to keep pushing themselves outside of their comfort zones. That's not news, but it's the truth. Foreign cultures can be bewildering—people behave differently, local customs seldom make sense. It's the same anywhere, but especially so in Japan and other parts of Asia where the culture is so deep and so different from the West. No matter how long I live in Japan, I don't think I'll ever completely grasp all the cultural nuances. There are times when the idiosyncracies are just too inexplicable, too hard to grasp.

At worst, I'd act out by playing up my status as an ugly American—disobeying pedestrian rules, ignoring proper social protocols even when I recognized the cues. If I was in a situation that demanded I use formal speech (keigo) to greet someone important, I'd blurt out the equivalent of "Yo." Another thing that Americans did was ride the train with inadequate train fare. Back in those days, they didn't have ticket machines, just ticket takers with hole punchers that the guys would swing in their hands, making a clackety-clack sound. I'd walk past the guy and give him my ticket with insufficient money on it, and he'd shout after me, and I'd pretend that I didn't understand him. They'd always let you go, because they figured you wouldn't understand what they had to say anyway. (Come to think of it, that's not really an ignored social cue, it's just outright theft.)

Something would always snap me back from my ugliness, though. I'd be lost and someone would put me in their car and take me home, make me dinner, and then drive me wherever I needed to go. The Japanese never failed to prove their unflagging generosity.

Japan can be a terribly frustrating country for a Westerner to fit into. Tokyo in the 1980s was a far less cosmopolitan place than it is now. People would see a white guy like me and be amazed by the smallest achievements. They'd compliment me for the most mundane stuff, like using chopsticks. For someone who was trying to blend in, it was deflating to be singled out for such dumb shit. In America, everybody assumes you understand English, because English is what you're supposed to understand. There's an expectation that you should acclimate, that you should speak the language. It can manifest itself in ugly, xenophobic ways, but it also means that if you learn to act like an American, people will treat you like one.

I'm essentially an adventurous person and I've always veered toward the unconventional, so I pushed myself. It was difficult to find situations that were conducive to learning, but I always challenged myself to go on day trips with Japanese speakers, or go drinking with Japanese acquaintances. Every now and then, I'd happen upon someone soldiering through the same challenges. One day I met a guy in front of a supermarket who was obviously an English speaker forcing himself to speak Japanese. We struggled through a broken conversation in Japanese—both of us refusing to resort to our native language. Our stubbornness made it ten times harder to get to know each other, but neither of us wanted to be seen as a gaijin, which translates as "outsider."

Nowadays I can call myself a gaijin in a self-effacing way, but back then it was hurtful to hear the word, to have my efforts to assimilate be dismissed. This guy and I both had the same goal; both of us wanted to find our own way in Japan on our own terms. Neither of us was seeking the easy solace of a gaijin friend.

None of this is to say that I was a model traveler, or that I got it right off the bat. In fact, I was a total wimp. Some of my fellow teachers would spend their earnings on trips to different parts of Japan, but not me. Nine months in, as soon as I'd saved up a little money, I flew right back home to New York.

I was homesick. This was before the Internet (no NPR, no *New York Times*), and international phone calls were $3 a minute. I missed my parents and my friends. I missed eating ice cream and going to the movies. Deli. New York pizza. Dim sum. Every time I came up with another $1,000 I would always fly back to New York. In retrospect, allowing myself to come back was the worst thing I could have done. While other people were saving their money to travel to Thailand or Nepal, or hitchhiking all over Japan, I would fly home and sit around in my parents' apartment—they'd moved to the Upper West Side—and drink coffee.

But to my credit, I always returned to Japan. The closest I ever came to staying was on one longer trip home. I'd been in the States for about two and a half months, and I'd become involved with a woman who wanted me to start a life with her in America. She didn't like Japan—she thought it was a misogynistic culture—and she tried to convince me to attend business school. Me, in a math-based graduate program! She almost succeeded, too. On a lark, I agreed to help her move across the country, and found myself with her in Maine. Then I had an epiphany. I looked up and said, "You know what? I don't like Maine and I love Japan. I don't know what the fuck you're talking about, but that's the place I want to be." No offense to Maine, but it took being there for me to realize how much I wanted to be somewhere else.

Each day in Japan yielded a new experience. One afternoon a Japanese friend dragged me to a hole-in-the-wall restaurant in Shibuya. It was four or five blocks from where I was working, in a stinky, dilapidated strip of restaurants. The place served all sorts of dishes—grilled saba (mackerel), katsudon (egg and pork cutlet over rice), that sort of thing—and ramen. Up to this point, I'd been sampling everything the local teishokus had to offer, but hadn't yet tried ramen. My friend sat me down and ordered us two bowls of miso ramen. That was the day I learned how to sweat.

This pungent, fatty soup landed in front of me. Currents of hot broth circulated around the bowl as if it was still simmering over a burner. I inhaled the steam tentatively, but my friend, hunched over his own bowl, insisted that I start eating immediately. He showed me how to gather a clump of noodles with my chopsticks and slurp them loudly into my mouth, followed by a spoonful of the scalding broth. It's hard to convey the pain of that first bite. It didn't just burn like hot pizza on the roof of your mouth. A layer of fat hovering on top of the soup seemed to have sucked in the flames from the stove only to unleash them in my head. I felt pins and needles pricking every surface of my face. My brain screamed for me to stop eating, but I looked around at all the other diners casually spooning and sucking in the boiling liquid, and I persevered.

I wouldn't say it was pleasant, but it was life affirming to be shocked out of my comfort zone. I became a regular, visiting the shop at least once a week for the three years I taught English in Shibuya. I learned to endure and eventually enjoy the heat, and appreciate the nuanced flavor behind it—intensely meaty and savory, but with subtle ripples of other

tastes that kept me slurping curiously. It'd be a little too romantic to say that I was instantly obsessed with ramen, or that I knew I'd somehow found my life's calling. At the time, that first bowl was just another in a long series of wonderfully bewildering encounters with Japanese culture.

The most profound of these encounters occurred a while later, at the end of my second year in Tokyo, when I met a gorgeous and sophisticated Japanese woman named Tami. She was a student of mine at Berlitz, learning to speak English so she could sell computer chips in the States. I wasn't exactly a playboy, but it wasn't that hard for American English teachers to land dates with Japanese girls. My first date with Tami was in December of 1988.

She took me to this club, essentially a big izakaya in the basement of an office building. I'd brought my English-to-Japanese dictionary and she had her Japanese-to-English one, and we sat there desperately trying to communicate with one another. I was definitely pursuing her, and I think she was intrigued, but all the nuance of flirting was impossible. In spite of the language barrier, we clicked. She was an extremely sophisticated Tokyo girl, but the charming awkwardness of the situation worked to my favor. We saw each other constantly for the next few months, and I fell in love with her.

But by the time I'd met her, Tami was already preparing to move to San Francisco to help open a new branch of the computer company she worked for. The only upside to Tami's leaving was that I finally landed a real job, working for her boss in Tokyo. With Tami gone, he hired me to help sell DRAM. To this day, I barely know what DRAM is, but I sold it for more than a year.

I had finally met someone who made me feel like I belonged in Japan, and now she was gone. For the first time, I felt stuck in Japan. I grew restless. My boss would take me drinking with his clients, parading me around as his gaijin, but he sensed my discontent. One day he stepped in and saved me: "Why don't you just go work with Tami in San Francisco?" I wasn't done with Japan, but I wasn't getting anywhere pining after Tami all day. I accepted the offer and just like that, nearly three years after it began, my first trip to Japan came to a close. I moved in with Tami in Mountain View, which wasn't exactly something that she'd planned on, but thankfully she agreed to take me in.

We quickly began building a pleasant little existence for ourselves in California, doing our best to maintain a Japanese lifestyle. We spoke a hybrid of Japanese and English, ate Japanese food and watched Japanese TV. Professionally, though, I was in a rut. I was still working for Tami's company, selling computer parts I didn't understand. I'd think wist-fully, but not really practically, about cooking. And so, while I'd fled the monotony and restlessness of Tokyo, I was still just a rudderless young man—now in California.

I was bummed out and irritable. I called my dad one day and moped, "I don't know what to do with my life. I'm unhappy and I don't know what I want to do—"

"Get a hold of yourself—you're a grown man," he replied. "Get your shit together." He then proceeded to dress me down for a while, until finally, almost out of nowhere, I blurted out, "You know, I was sort of thinking that maybe I should go to culinary school."

For years, my parents had been somewhat ambivalent about my fascination with food. Sometimes they'd see it as an attention-grabbing ploy of mine, an attempt to come off as interesting. Other times they'd indulge me, and suggest that if I liked food so much, I should find a career in it.

My dad paused for a second and said, "Your mother and I had the same thought the other day. You should go."

A Cook's Life

It was the summer of 1991. I wasn't anything close to a professional cook; I was just a guy in his late twenties who loved food. This was years before *Kitchen Confidential* made cooking seem like a badass—let alone respectable—occupation.

To be fair, my parents would never have objected if I'd told them I wanted to go to culinary school straight out of high school, but back then, when I thought about the long hours and toil of cooking, I just wasn't ready. But in California I found myself at a crossroads, and I felt like time was running out for me to commit to something. Why not bite the bullet and choose to pursue something I actually enjoyed?

Nowadays, there are hundreds and hundreds of cooking schools to choose from, and more than enough has been written about what it's like to be a culinary student, a cook, and a chef. When I was looking to get into the business, however, there were only a few options. I applied to the Culinary Institute of America in New York, got in, and moved back east with Tami. We got married on May 10, 1992.

The curriculum at CIA was focused almost exclusively on French, Austrian, and German technique. Back then, as far as cooking schools were

concerned, the only people who knew how to cook were French and German people. I sucked at cooking school, just like I sucked at regular school. As exciting as it was to be thinking about and tinkering with food every day, I was still the same obstinate student I'd always been. I irritated my classmates (a bunch of rednecks, I thought), and after a few weeks almost no one was speaking to me. I didn't even attend my own graduation. But I'm still glad I went. It gave me my first taste of cooking in professional kitchens, and I loved it.

While I was still in school, I got an externship at Bobby Flay's Mesa Grill, and for a brief time I was part of the hottest new restaurant in New York. Flay was a superb manager, working with his staff in a way that made a huge impression on me. He never yelled, and when he was angry he took care of it privately. He had good advice for me: "Keep your mouth shut, pay attention, help out wherever you can, and everyone will want to teach you." The cooks were all tremendously talented. It wasn't until I was in that kitchen that I really began to understand the fundamentals of cooking—seasoning, grilling, roasting, braising, sautéing.

After graduation in 1993, most of my classmates sought out jobs at fine-dining places in Manhattan. I had a friend who went to Le Bernardin, another who went to Daniel. I got a dream job: Lutèce, one of the greatest French restaurants in the United States—a *Times* four-star restaurant for almost thirty years, with virtually no turnover in staff. When I was a little kid, my parents told me that

Top left: Cooking Thanksgiving dinner at my sister's house, with my son Isaac looking on. **Top right:** Becoming a cook generally means you absorb all the home-cooking duties, too. **Bottom left:** Me, with a massive basket of chanterelles that I found behind my house in Woodstock, where I lived during my CIA days. **Bottom right:** I was too cheap to buy school portraits at CIA, so I stole the outtake shots. This is the only photographic evidence I have that I went to cooking school.

Lutèce was the best restaurant in New York. Whenever they'd take us out to eat, without fail I'd say, "Can we go to Lutèce?!" Of course, we never did, but it still felt like I was coming full circle when I got the job there. Nobody in my family could believe it.

At Lutèce, I was surrounded by outstanding cooks who were mature and confident enough to share their wisdom and advice. My job was to assist the sous chef, Bill Peet (who remains a great friend and source of inspiration). But the most important lessons I learned at Lutèce were about hospitality. Lutèce was like no other restaurant in the country for one simple reason: André Soltner, the chef and proprietor. Soltner was king of the New York fine-dining scene. Heads of state, movie stars—they all flocked to Lutèce. Every day, at the beginning of both lunch and dinner service, he would be waiting at the door in a stark white chef's jacket, a neckerchief crisply knotted around his neck, greeting customers as they came in. Every morning he was in promptly at nine, without fail. At early morning sessions, he would check the reservations and make sure we were prepared for his regulars: Mrs. S loves steak tartare; Mr. Head-of-a-Large-Corporation wants apple tart—be sure to have one ready.

I spent two transformative years at Lutèce. When it was time for a change in scenery, I started cooking all around Manhattan. All the stories that had made me apprehensive about the restaurant business were true: the grueling hours, burns and cuts, screaming chefs, coming home greasy and stinking of fish. But I also acquired a skill that I had sorely lacked my entire life: I learned how to suck it up. The Japanese refer to this notion as *gaman*, and it's a skill that is absolutely necessary to survive more than five minutes in a professional kitchen.

Most surprisingly, I found that I loved it. I loved the intensity. I loved having to do twenty things at once. I loved the pace. Pushing through pain was exhilarating. I'd traded in my confused, meandering days for ones filled with purpose. That's what's great about cooking: you focus on the task at hand, and then you move on to the next one. You're too busy to get lost in your own thoughts or feel sorry for yourself.

But line cooking is a young man's game. I was in my thirties. I was married. And in 1996, I became a father. Tami gave birth to our son, Isaac, in February of that year, on what turned out to be the most wonderful day of my life.

While Tami was pregnant with Isaac, I interviewed for a line-cook job at Union Square Cafe. The chef was also fascinated with Japan, and we had an interesting conversation. I did a trial and he offered me the main sauté position. The pay was $400 a week gross, meaning $250 take-home, with no benefits to speak of. I wanted to continue moving up the cooking ladder, but now I had a family to support. I thanked the chef, but told him I just couldn't live on $250 a week.

So I went corporate.

I started working for Restaurant Associates, a well-known restaurant company that also provides corporate dining services for businesses and museums. Cafeterias ranging from upscale to downscale—that sort of thing. I became the executive chef for a boutique investment firm. My work schedule went from long nights, weekends, and holidays, six days a week, to a predictable 6 a.m. to 2 p.m., Mondays through Fridays, with insurance, bonuses, and an expense account. My little café served breakfast and lunch to 250 every day, and was a safe zone for a lot of stressed-out people. In that environment, it dawned on me how much food means to people. I listened to complaints, I built trust, and I did my best to make everyone happy. I nurtured a feeling of warmth in the dining room, and served the most delicious food I could.

Isaac was born a month or two after I started at the firm. Fine-dining restaurants don't ordinarily have enough money to take care of their staffs—it's just a fact of the business. Many chefs and owners would love to pay a guy for paternity leave, or let him stay home to watch the kids while his wife is sick, but they just can't; there's enough money for one salary, and if you can't come in, they have to find someone else. But Restaurant Associates gave me a week off when my son was born, a luxury that most restaurants would balk at, especially for a new hire.

Sometimes I think back and wish I'd sucked it up a little longer and taken that job at Union Square Cafe, or worked at another place and built up my cooking chops a bit more. I wonder if I could've used another year or two of toughening up. There are a lot of wonderful things about working in a premier restaurant in New York. When things are clicking, you're turning out great food and the newspapers are all singing your praises. If you're on a good team, there's an inimitable camaraderie. Like any fine-dining cook, I daydreamed about running my own kitchen and cooking my own food. As a chef now, I still feel defensive about my decision to leave the grind for a corporate dining job. But I made a tough choice for my family, and ultimately, it was the right one.

Things were humming along. Life was never better. I was settled at work and at home. Isaac had turned two, and Tami was five months pregnant with our second child. We'd just sold our apartment and were preparing to move into a cute three-bedroom house with a backyard in Mamaroneck.

My immediate family all lived close by. Our apartment was stocked to the ceiling with boxes in preparation for the move.

Then, in three short days, my entire world crashed down around me.

On a Tuesday, Tami went to a trade show at the Javits Center and came home with a chill. Over the phone, the obstetrician recommended she just try to get some rest, but her condition continued to worsen. We finally talked the doctor into seeing us at the hospital. When we got there, they admitted Tami into the obstetrics department rather than emergency—which turned out to be a tragic mistake. By noon on Friday, she had miscarried—we lost our daughter. Within another hour, Tami's condition had deteriorated even further. One after another, her organs began shutting down. She went into a coma at three in the afternoon. The inexperienced obstetrician hadn't recognized the signs of toxic shock, and now it was too late. I went home and held Isaac and cried myself to sleep. Tami passed away the next day.

She was the first woman I'd ever loved, and I think she was the first to ever love me. Until we met, I had always been rebellious, immature, and unsettled. She was powerful, decisive, and focused, and she made up for

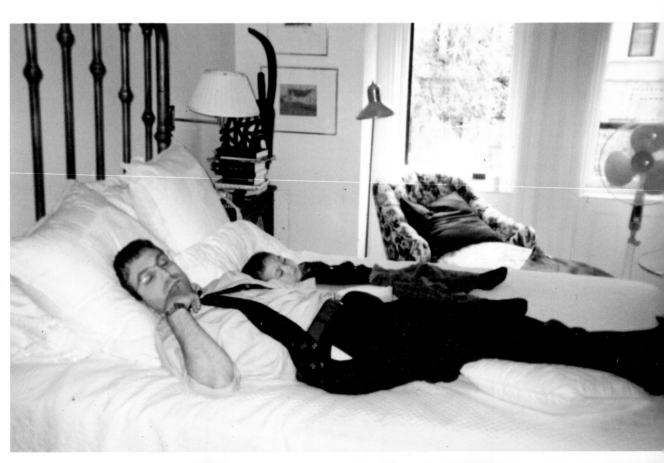

all the things that I lacked. In the ten years we'd been together, I'd gone from being a confused, aimless kid in Tokyo to a husband, a father, and a chef. Losing Tami was devastating. In a horrifying flash, I'd become a single dad grieving the loss of his wife and unborn daughter.

But I was also in the best situation one could hope for under such terrible circumstances. The truth is that much worse things happen to people who are less well equipped to cope with loss. I still had a beautiful, healthy son and owned a nice apartment. I worked a steady job for a company that gave me time off to sort out my life. I could afford a nanny, and my parents lived down the block. I would walk over there every day and have meals with them, and they would help with the kid.

I was brokenhearted, but tried to remain grateful and strong for Isaac, who had just lost as much as I had, if not more. I like to think I rose to the occasion. I reinvented myself for him and, thanks to my supportive family, we both slowly recovered. Learning to adapt after Tami's death made me into a man. Being a single father beat any lingering irresponsibility out of me. After a couple of years went by, I began to feel the rhythm of life as a single parent.

The one thing I couldn't replace was our family's cultural connection to Japan. With Tami gone, I missed the Japanese part of my life. We had spoken Japanese in the house, and our home had a Japanese energy to it. I wanted Isaac to have that culture in his life. So six months after Tami passed, I made my first extended trip back to Japan in almost ten years.

Left: The worst day of my life. Isaac and me, asleep after Tami's funeral.

The Obsession

Over the next few years, I continued to visit Japan every nine months or so. I'd bring Isaac to see his grandparents, and we'd stay with Eric in Tokyo.

On one of those trips, four years after Tami died, a friend wanted to introduce us to her friend Mari, who was also raising a son on her own. When Tami died, I'd spent a year single and completely uninterested in dating. After that, I began easing back into things. Dating after your wife dies is not exactly easy, especially when you have a little kid. In the year before I met Mari, I'd been dating a lot, meeting a lot of women, but failing to make any sort of real connection. A few months before the trip to Japan, I decided to stop casually dating, and wait until I found someone I really liked. So it was with that in mind that I cautiously agreed to meet Mari and her son, Alex.

Isaac and I met them at a park in Tokyo. After a few hours of chatting while the kids played in the park, I asked Mari and Alex to dinner. The first meal we had together was at a famous garlic tonkotsu (fatty, sticky pork broth) ramen shop. It's still around. These days, I find the soup there too garlicky and fatty, but back then I thought it was really great—intense and rich and porky. Plus, I was there with Mari and Isaac and Alex; our afternoon blind date had bled over into the night.

Isaac and I ended up spending the rest of our time in Tokyo with Mari and Alex. When we returned home to New York, I was miserable. I couldn't stop thinking about Mari. I called her, and we talked about how ridiculous it felt to let distance keep us from being together. I decided that I had to go back to Japan. My parents thought I was insane. I told them I'd met someone. "You were just there a week ago," they said. I told them I needed to see her again.

A few days later, I dropped Isaac off at their house. They were furious. I was being reckless, impetuous. My mom told me she refused to take care of Isaac just so I could go meet some girl halfway around the world. But I didn't back down. This was my first real glimpse of romantic love in four years. Mari and I had chemistry, and I'm big on chemistry. I told my parents the same thing I'd been telling them all my life: "I'm not asking for your permission— I'm just letting you know." Eventually, they relented and I left for Tokyo.

I spent four days in Japan. I met Mari's parents and brother and professed my love for her. We were together the entire time, and made plans to see each other the next month in New York. On August 10, 2002—a little less than three months from the day we met—we were married. Mari decorated my parents' house with flowers she bought in the flower district, and I planned the menu and cooked the food with the help of some friends. We crammed seventy people into the house, and it was a truly joyous day. I was surrounded by friends and family who had stood by my side through the low moments of the previous four years. To have them with me as I came full circle was immensely moving.

After the wedding, we tried to settle into life in New York. Thankfully, our kids got along right away—Alex, who was two years old, worshipped his new older brother. I was in my seventh year working for Restaurant Associates. The first four or five years had been wonderful. I didn't have to worry about profits or losses; I just had to make customers happy, and there were no corporate games to play. Then a big conglomerate bought the company, and the warm, fuzzy feeling began to dissipate. The economy started to tank, and suddenly I had to get with the program, work different hours, and cook whatever they asked me to. It began when they'd given me a hard time about taking a Sunday off for my wedding, and continued with my boss squeezing me into doing stuff I didn't want to do—special events like taco day and Mardi Gras day—along with more and more paperwork.

Unlike many people I'd met in Japan, Mari had never aspired to live in New York. And yet here she was, living in a house filled with my late wife's possessions. I hadn't felt the need to clear anything out before she moved in, nor am I sure I could have. So now whenever Mari opened a closet or a drawer, there were Tami's things. Everyone loved Mari and completely

Right: Alex, Issac, and me in Tokyo, with the cherry blossoms in full bloom.

accepted her into our family, but friends and relatives would sometimes inadvertently call her by my dead wife's name. It was beyond awkward and terribly painful for all of us.

Nine months after the wedding, we took our first trip to Japan as a family. Our arrival coincided with the first cherry blossoms opening. I found myself sitting with my sons and wife on Daigaku-Dori, a famous street in Kunitachi with cherry trees on either side of the roadway—it's stunning. We were admiring the blossoms, and all at once I was overwhelmed by a desire to live in Japan again—this time as a fully functioning adult. I'd just turned forty, and it felt like it was now or never. I told Mari what I was thinking, and she said, "If we move to Japan, you realize that you'll probably never live in New York again, right?" When I asked her why, she said, "Well, say that in ten years you decide you want to go back and start over in New York. You'll be fifty. How are you going to restart your life when you're fifty?" I said, "If it ends up that we never move back to New York, I'm willing to live with it." And so it was that, about a year after getting married, I was living in Tokyo once again.

Mari had enough well-paid work to support all of us in Tokyo. I spent my days taking care of the family and occasionally helping Mari with her projects. I woke up at 6:30, made the kids breakfast, and packed their lunches. I did the shopping and made dinner. I shuttled my wife around while she bought props and other materials for her work. In the back of my mind, I wondered if I could continue my cooking career in Japan, but mostly I was content just to raise the kids and live in Tokyo.

In America, I'd come to miss so many of Japan's offerings. Some things had trickled over to New York, but others never made it. Over the years, it had become possible to find passable Japanese ingredients and even great sushi in the States, but decent ramen was nonexistent. My desire for the stuff had grown into a fixation. It was a real you-don't-know-what-you've-got-till-it's-gone situation.

To my surprise, when I returned to Tokyo ravenous for a bowl, ramen had changed—for the better. When I'd first tried ramen years earlier, it was light-years ahead of the instant stuff in America, but it was still just fast food. Huge corporate chains produced noodles in factories and shipped them in plastic to outlets where they were dumped into pots of boiling water.

Then a few pioneering cooks began meticulously crafting bowls of kodawari (the word means something like "artisanal") ramen—handcrafted stuff, with high-quality ingredients and careful attention to detail. Specially sourced chickens and pigs, salt produced on a tiny island off the coast of Okinawa, small-batch soy sauce, water filtered through complex charcoal systems—that sort of thing. People were treating ramen making as a craft.

Soon, ramen celebrities started cropping up. One of these was a man named Sano-san, who made his name as a TV personality in the late nineties. His show was called Ramen Oni, "The Ramen Devil." Aspiring ramen cooks would subject themselves to his tutelage and criticism. In return, he'd reduce the young ramenistas to tears. He made Gordon Ramsay look like a teddy bear. At the end of the season, the one contestant who demonstrated the most steadfastness was honored with Sano-san's blessing and assistance in opening his own shop.

I'd actually eaten at Sano-san's shop in 2000, before I'd ever seen his show. The shop had very strict rules: no talking, no cell phones, no babies, no perfume. The customers seemed to cower as they silently filed into the shop. Each customer was given a color-coded chip after ordering and paying outside. They'd place the chip on the counter without a word, then await their food. The shop was pristine, like a sushi bar. Everyone ate silently. If you needed to use the restroom, you'd tip-toe.

As we ate, we occasionally looked up and nodded to one another in approval. Then we shuffled out quietly, bowing a thank you and exiting as wordlessly as we'd entered. It was one of the stranger, more uncomfortable dining experiences of my life, but it was also revelatory—the best bowl of ramen I'd ever eaten.

When we moved back to Tokyo, finding more ramen like that became a personal quest for me. On Mari's days off, we'd boot up a cellphone app called Ramen Navi and start driving. Ramen Navi included a huge database of great ramen shops all over Tokyo. In that first year back in Tokyo, I was probably eating at three different ramen shops each week.

Some places were duds. We went to a hoity-toity dashi-based shop where the guy used a bamboo whisk intended for matcha tea to stir his dashi; every time he flicked his wrist, he'd splash us with soup. His shop was too precious, and his soup just wasn't very good. On the other hand, there was a place near my kids' school—what you'd refer to as an otaku, a "geek" shop, where the proprietors are meticulous (bordering on obsessive) about their product. The place was well known for serving a great handcrafted bowl of noodles. The chef made a shio (salt) ramen accented with shiso leaves, and it was just sublime. I must have eaten there at least twenty-five times. It was the first place I encountered the double soup.

The double soup was a relatively new creation, wherein the chef would make two separate broths—dashi, pork, chicken, whatever—and combine them only upon serving. The result was a lighter soup, with really clean, forward flavors. It was the opposite of varieties like tonkotsu, which are thick, fatty broths made by cooking the hell out of pork bones. More importantly, in my eyes double soup represented a sea change in the way ramen was being made and perceived. It wasn't just fast food anymore. People were applying real technique and serious thought to once-simple bowls. Nobody considered it to be on the same level as sushi or formal kaiseki cuisine, but it was certainly taking strides forward.

Ramen was the sort of food I loved to eat, now being made in the way I'd been trained to cook.

Answers from a Master: Shimazaki-San

My friend Shimazaki-san is a total trip. Every day he comes to work at his ramen shop in a bowling shirt and black pants, his hair slicked back like a greaser, with just one strand carefully allowed to hang over his forehead. He demands total silence from his diners, serves his soup in bowls with a nanotechnological polish, and sources his chickens from a specific prefecture. His ramen is a perfect example of the kodawari movement that grabbed my attention when I came back to Japan—ramen elevated to the level of fine cuisine, with great attention to detail and craft.

His strict no-talking policy has earned him a reputation as a gruff, no-nonsense guy. But he's one of the kindest, most generous chefs I've ever met. You notice it if you look closely. Watch his face while he methodically shakes and strains the water from his noodles, then silently whips around and carefully folds them over themselves into the bowl, then finally passes the bowl to you without a word. He's not unhappy to serve you, and often you'll even see him cracking a smile—he just wants you to get the most out of your meal.

I was a little worried about interrogating him for this book; it's not entirely polite in Japanese culture to ask blunt questions about people's methods and quirks, especially if you're talking to a well-respected person like Shimazaki-san. But he approached our conversation with earnest pleasure; I think he was happy to talk about the craft he loves.

Ivan Orkin: How long have you been working as a ramen chef?

Shimazaki-san: I don't feel like making ramen is really a job. I have a passion for ramen. By the time I was sixteen, I had worked in sixteen different restaurants with different cuisines. I was a student working at a ramen shop on the side, and an old guy there gave me the recipe for Tokyo ramen. At the end of the year, I invited my friends over and made a huge batch of ramen. As I was cooking the chicken soup, and the chicken fat started to bubble to the surface of the soup, I got goose bumps. I didn't know what it meant, but at the time, it felt like a sign.

IO: So it's not a job, it's a calling. What's in your bowl of ramen?

S: I express myself in my ramen. I try to see many different details and angles, and that helps me make a good bowl. There aren't many different recipes for ramen, so it's all in the small variations—temperature, water, process. Same ingredients, but different methods.

IO: Why's it important to you that your customers be silent while eating your ramen?

S: Three things. One, I can't concentrate on making ramen with too much noise. Two, as for the customer, if they're talking instead of eating, then the noodle expands in the broth; it has a short life. Three, the biggest reason is that if I hear customers having an interesting conversation, I want to join them. I'm actually very talkative.

IO: Do you think other restaurants should adopt that policy?

S: Each restaurant is different. If another chef wanted me to be silent, I'd obey.

IO: Did you invent this policy or did you adopt it from someone else?

S: I made it up. And since then, I've seen it in many ramen shops. I'm guessing there are some sushi restaurants with the same policy, but I haven't been to one myself.

IO: Tell me about the bowls.

S: I use porcelain from Atayaki, an area famous for its many porcelain companies. I ask for a very special lacquering process using nanotechnology, which creates a microscopic grain. You can taste the difference between bowls, and these bowls don't lose temperature as easily.

IO: Why do you have such a specific set of movements when you're straining your noodles?

S: The point is to shed as much hot water as possible. The alkaline water that comes off the noodle can dilute and compete with the soup's flavor. If you just go up and down, water is still stuck in the center of the noodles. When you switch to back and forth, more water comes out. So first comes the up and down, then I finish back and forth. Every single movement style is supposed to look cool. And the way I move reduces back pain, too.

IO: How long did it take to develop this style?

S: It came naturally, but I tried many styles. I don't allow my cooks to use the same style—I want them to develop their own style. I teach them how to hold the bowls, where to put the knife, but they should develop their own methods, too.

IO: Tell me about the chickens and the chicken fat.

S: The chicken is from Akita prefecture, and is one of the three most famous chicken breeds in Japan. How they raise them, the feed, and how long they grow them are all important. I tried many different types before choosing this one. I thought, "Even if I use bad chickens, I should be able to make a good soup. If not, I shouldn't be allowed to use this famous, expensive chicken."

IO: When you place the noodles in the bowl, you pick them back up and rearrange them very specifically with the chopsticks. Why?

S: I want to make it look beautiful and easy for the customers to pick up. I hand them the noodles pointing in the same direction every time. The way things appear, the beauty, is very significant.

IO: How long do you work on a new menu?

S: Sometimes three years for a whole menu.

IO: Americans see Japanese cuisine as very particular and detail-oriented like yours. Is that accurate?

S: It's funny, because there are so many places in Japan that aren't like that. I want my ramen to be at the top of the line, higher even. Ramen should surprise the customer. I don't think about other ramen shops first—I think about my own way. My purpose is just to have customers say my ramen is delicious. I like to hear that.

IO: Do you enjoy other styles of ramen, ramen that's not so precise?

S: I think there's a relationship between that type of ramen and this one. But I like serious ramen cooks; even if the ramen doesn't taste great, I respect the seriousness. I care about the passion. My private style is more messy; it's only with ramen that I care about the small details.

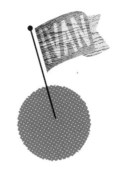

So?

We'd been living in Japan for three years. I was doing a lot of putzing around, eating ramen, watching *Grey's Anatomy*, wasting time on the Internet, and reading tons of newspapers and magazines. I was growing irritable, maybe even resentful.

Finally, one day Mari turned to me and said, "You can do whatever you want, but you look bored and miserable. If you ask me, it's time for you to *do* something." She was right. I loved taking care of the family, but with Mari's flexible work hours we could easily share the responsibility. I hadn't come to Japan to sit on my ass.

For years, I'd been building a running list in my head of things I would do if I had my own restaurant. The kids were now old enough that a place of my own was a logistical possibility. And so began a number of epic discussions about what kind of restaurant to open. My experience was in fine dining, especially French and regional American cuisine. But Tokyo already had great French food. Come to think of it, they had great Italian and Chinese food, too. Skilled, open-minded cooks were traveling from Japan to train in Michelin-starred European kitchens, then returning to ply their trades. I didn't want to get into the fine-dining game with them.

It may have been in the back of my head, but Mari was the one who put it into words. "How about ramen?" she said. "You love it, and there's not one American making ramen in Japan, so you've got an angle."

Of course I was crazy about ramen, and I desperately wanted to try making my own. But I wasn't sold on the idea of opening a ramen shop. An American making ramen in the middle of Tokyo felt more like a parlor trick than a viable plan.

We decided to embark on a whirlwind trip to New York, Paris, and Hawaii, eating our way around the world. Maybe we'd get some clarity by seeing what people were doing around the world. In New York, we ate at Momofuku Noodle Bar. I distinctly remember feeling jealous. Here was David Chang, a Korean-American who'd also identified how special ramen is, opened his own shop, and was doing great with it.

Over the course of the rest of the trip, we ate at some incredible restaurants. We ate at some incredibly bad places, too. I started thinking about what it would mean to open an American restaurant in Tokyo. American chefs like to look at different cuisines and reinterpret them using local ingredients. Like, "I really like this Spanish dish so maybe I'll make my version using ingredients from Tsukiji fish market—it'll be Ivan Orkin's twisted American tapas." That's what it means to cook American cuisine in New York or Seattle or San Francisco, but I didn't think that that would sell in Tokyo. Japanese people would say, "Where are the pizza, hot dogs, and hamburgers?"—that's what people think of as American food here. I thought about opening a sandwich shop, but my wife reminded me that meat is expensive in Tokyo. To serve a decent sandwich, I'd have to charge $20, and nobody in Tokyo was going to spend that.

Mari kept coming back to the ramen idea, and kept hammering away at my reservations. Finally, one day we went for a bowl at a famous noodle shop and had an incredibly disappointing experience. I was moaning and groaning on our way out the door about how much better I could do it.

"So?" Mari asked.

My mother-in-law is something of a feng shui fanatic. She's not concerned with how we arrange our furniture, but she likes to tell us where to go and where to avoid going: "If you walk east every day for a month, you will increase good fortune," and all that. One year, when we wanted to take

Right: The shopping arcade in Rokakoen where Ivan Ramen is located—one of the few locations that my mother-in-law approved of.

a vacation to New Zealand, she put the kibosh on it, saying, "No, that's a terrible direction; terrible things will happen to you." When I decided to open my own ramen shop, she blocked out a couple square miles where I was allowed to look. A lot of people ask me why I chose an out-of-the-way suburban neighborhood for my shop. The simple answer is that my mother-in-law told me to.

However, in the beginning finding a location was the least of my concerns. I'd never cooked a bowl of ramen in my life. I was an American transplant in Tokyo, trying to break into a notoriously insular culinary culture. I hadn't cooked professionally in three years, and I'd never owned my own restaurant. Even today, I still believe I could have used another ten years working in fine-dining restaurants before opening my own spot.

What I did have going for me was the freedom to fail. I wasn't under any tremendous pressure to succeed; my wife had a good job that had already supported us for three years. When I told my dad that I was thinking of opening a ramen shop, he asked how much I could sell a bowl of ramen for. "Seven or eight bucks," I told him.

"How the hell are you going to make any money doing that?"

"Sell a lot of bowls, I guess."

Not many people have the luxury of opening a business just because they're passionate about something. I was opening a ramen shop because I loved ramen.

As it turns out, ramen was a fortuitous choice. Ramen is a maverick cuisine—every shop is run differently. Of all the principal Japanese cuisines—sushi, soba, kaiseki, washoku—ramen is the most open, the most receptive to change and experimentation. It's probably the only Japanese cuisine I could have succeeded in as an outsider. The training period for the average sushi chef is three years. Many sushi places won't even let you touch the rice during your first two years; you wash dishes, mop the floor, fetch things, and just watch. There are still places that say women can't be sushi chefs because their body temperature is lower than men's. It's a guarded, unbending culture that's difficult to penetrate, let alone succeed in.

Kaiseki—Japanese haute cuisine—is equally rigid. With each change of the seasons, you have a different set of dishes you're supposed to make. Each dish has a specific plate it's supposed to be served on. Kaiseki chefs have told me that it can cost upward of $100,000 for a restaurant just to change out all the plates and bowls every year.

Being a good sushi or tempura or yakitori chef is about endless repetition. They're slicing fish, frying vegetables, grilling meat. They're just really, really good at it. When I watch a sushi chef or a tempura chef, I can see everything that's going on. He's dipping the vegetables in batter, and now he's frying it; or he's got some warm rice and he's putting some sliced fish on it. It's all very simple; the beauty and difficulty are in the execution. On the other hand, when I'd watch a ramen chef, I'd wonder what the hell he was doing, what he was ladling from those mystery containers, why he did what he did. A large part of why I ultimately decided to make ramen is that I was desperately curious about how it was done.

We started with the basics. Mari and I attended the first annual World Ramen Expo in Yokohama. The Expo wasn't exactly a gathering of artisanal ramen makers—more like a trade show, big companies peddling premade chashu (roast pork) and tare (seasoning). But it was a start. I met a representative from Yamato, a noodle-machine manufacturer I'd read about online. He told me that the company offered a six-day crash course for people interested in opening ramen shops. I figured, what the hell? If I was going to drop $100,000 opening a ramen shop, there was no shame in taking a beginner course first.

Whenever I'd imagine making my own ramen, I'd get stuck on how the Japanese put so much flavor into their soup. The flavorful soups I knew were consommés, or purees, or flavorful stocks that you'd swirl pesto into. But this was a whole new animal. Like any good dish, for ramen to be delicious it needs two things: well-made components and perfect harmony. But because the elements that make up a bowl of ramen have such strong flavors—pork, smoked fish, soy sauce, salt—it's easy to let the strong flavors overpower the lighter ones. I couldn't understand how ramen broth had so much clear, distinct flavor.

The ramen class was taught by noncooks, but they knew how a bowl of ramen was constructed. They taught me the fundamentals of making a ramen-style soup. I learned a little about dashi, and the function of fat—why and how it's added—in ramen broth. I listened and asked a lot of questions, and silently thought about the changes I'd make. All my ramen eating had given me a clear idea of the flavor profile I wanted in my soup. A lot of ramen is strongly flavored from the first bite and can be overpowering by the end of the bowl. I think the inverse is smarter, building flavor to a climax at the end. I wanted to layer flavors, deploying the same tastes in several different guises—chicken broth plus chicken fat, for example. The idea would be to keep recognizable flavors hitting you in waves from different directions. The class provided me with a rudimentary roadmap to creating that effect.

Almost exactly one year passed between the day we said, "Let's start a ramen shop," and the day we opened the doors of Ivan Ramen.

Every day of that year I wondered if I should apprentice with a ramen chef. But being as old as I was, with the amount of cooking experience I had, I really didn't have it in me to take on a one- or two-year apprenticeship. Ramen apprenticeships were generally for people with no cooking experience, more interested in a job than in the craft. Most people graduate apprenticeships only to open an identical shop to their master's. I didn't want to be disrespectful and approach a guy and say, "Oh please, teach me what you do," and then bail after three months to open my own place. But I gave it serious consideration. There were multiple times when I walked into a ramen shop, hat in hand, ready to ask the owner about an apprentice position. But the words never came out. At the end of the day, I thought, "Fuck it, I'm a good cook, I can figure it out for myself."

The ramen course had removed the crucial obstacle of not knowing a damn thing about anything. After that, I upped the frequency and studiousness of my ramen-shop visits. I'd walk in, eat a bowl of ramen, and take mental notes about flavor, presentation, service, atmosphere, types of stools, bowls, chopsticks, background music—anything I could glean. Ramen shops can be cryptic. The signs didn't entirely make sense, and I couldn't see what was going on behind the counter, what they were dipping ladles into, or what the numbers on their noodle-cooking timers said. Ramen cooks are generally silent when they're working, and the menus aren't terribly descriptive; plus, at that my point my knowledge of kanji (Japanese characters) wasn't what it is today.

Still, I was always watching. I knew the gist of what was going on, and I was picking up information bit by bit. Finally, I came home with what I thought was a good set of recipes. They weren't my recipes, but I thought they'd make a bowl of ramen like we'd eaten at any number of restaurants. I made a bowl for Mari and she said, "This is garbage. You're a good cook and a smart guy. Don't make other people's food. Go back and figure out what you want to cook, and make your own food."

I knew I wanted to make a double-soup shio ramen. I would keep the broth light and the taste clear, incorporating flavors that appealed to me. I tinkered obsessively in our tiny Tokyo kitchen, trying to come up with a bowl that reflected my personal point of view, while remaining faithful to the qualities I'd fallen in love with. I was reading a lot of ramen cookbooks, and I would constantly run through ideas and recipes in my head.

Every serious Japanese soba shop makes its own noodles by hand. The most serious chefs go so far as to plant their own buckwheat, harvest it, and grind it to ensure the highest level of product. Not so with ramen shops, where noodles take a distant backseat to the soup and the chashu. In fact, most shops order their noodles from a manufacturer. It made no sense to me to put so much time and effort into crafting a perfect bowl of soup and accompaniments, just to let someone else drive their noodle bus right through the bowl. I was going to make my own noodles—no question.

Ramen noodles are just flour, water, salt, and kansui—a bicarbonate that gives them their signature alkaline flavor and mouthfeel. Some places will also add whole eggs to their noodles for color and flavor and a little extra bite, but I find that it interferes with the wheat flavor. Without kansui, though, you've just got wheat noodles. A little kansui gives the noodles a unique aroma, a mild metallic tang, and most important a springiness, the characteristic dance the noodles do as you slurp and chew them.

Striking the right mix of flour, water, and kansui is a funky balance of science and craft. The more water you add, the chewier the noodle

becomes. Too much kansui, and you can end up with bitter noodles and crumbling structure. On rainy days, when there's more moisture in the air, the flour might take less water. But there's no substitute for experience. To get a perfect noodle recipe, you've got to try it over and over and over again. I tried dozens of flour combinations, making batch after batch of noodles on a $20 hand-crank pasta machine I'd bought in Little Italy years before.

What I was looking for was a noodle with flavor and bite (in Japanese, noodles with real chew are said to have "mochi mochi"), one that slurps smoothly and adheres to the soup. I made lots of noodles that tasted amazing on their own, but for whatever reason the soup just wouldn't stick to them. I didn't make my first complete bowl of ramen until three months before we opened, and I didn't actually finalize the noodle recipe until just a week before.

Meanwhile, we needed to start looking for a location. As I mentioned, my mother-in-law had demarcated a tiny area where we were allowed to look. We scoured the area for three months without luck. The realtors told me there was absolutely nothing available. Even when we expanded our

search to towns with six-figure populations, there was nothing. Ramen shops have a bad reputation. They're dirty, and smelly, and often have disreputable owners who suddenly decide to disappear on some miserable, customerless night. It's hard to convince real estate agents and building owners that you're going to be different, especially when you're a foreigner. Furthermore, a lot of places in Tokyo change hands many times without bothering with a realtor; some guy tells his friend he's thinking of moving out and then his friend scarfs up the space.

At the time, we were also eating our way through a ramen guidebook. One day we followed the book to a shop in a town called Rokakoen, just a ten-minute drive from our house, well within my mother-in-law's permissible area. The owner was a weathered, wiry five-foot-tall woman in her fifties with an exceedingly friendly demeanor. She made a classic Kyushu tonkotsu ramen with Hakata-style noodles—very thin noodles that cook in 20 to 30 seconds. She seasoned them with a few squirts of soy sauce and a sprinkle of MSG, then topped it off with pork soup. It wasn't bad, and the shop was pretty famous. The owner had gained some notoriety for starting out in a food truck, then graduating to this space.

It was a small shop, nothing fancy, with just enough space to make an honest bowl of ramen. It was located on a corner and had a nice L-shaped counter. The neighborhood was funky and interesting, the train station and a major highway were nearby, and it was close to home.

While sitting at the counter, eating a bowl of tonkotsu ramen, I mentioned to the owner that I intended to open my own ramen shop. As she removed my bowl, she said she was tired and thinking of retirement. She told me I could come help out in the shop, and that I would be her heir. When she retired, I could purchase the rights from her. I could be her new son, she told me, a wonderful and talented person who would take Tokyo by storm. I was thrilled, even if her invitation seemed a bit impulsive and erratic and possibly indicative of some more serious emotional instability. I generally feel suspicious of people who are too affectionate too quickly. I don't love being hugged by people I just met. I was wary of the owner taking me under her wing so quickly, but it was the first real lead I'd had, so I followed it.

I started coming in to help cut vegetables and cook and perform various odds-and-ends tasks, all without pay. Then, a month into our arrangement, she phoned me up and indignantly forbade me from returning to the shop. I was baffled. She didn't give any explanation, only that I was no longer welcome in the shop. I was distraught and confused, and had no idea what

I'd done, but I respected her wishes. Only much later did I find out that she'd taken great offense when I opened her refrigerator without permission. I'd wanted to see how she organized it, and apparently she considered that extremely rude.

So I didn't visit the shop for the better part of three months. Then one day Mari told me I should suck it up and see what was bothering the lady. I popped my head into the shop, and just as mysteriously as she'd turned on me, she gathered me back to her bosom. We were best buddies again. She said she was ready to retire, if I still wanted the shop. I'm not sure what changed her mind, but I have a hunch it was the money dangling in front of her. We made a deal for the space that week. In exchange for $20,000, she would hand over the restaurant and leave everything—the bowls, the noodle cookers, and the pots.

On March 1, 2007, I stood on the street, looking at an empty ramshackle little building in a quiet corner of Tokyo. The transfer hadn't come off as smoothly as we'd hoped. The owner had wanted me to give her friend a sweetheart contract as a carpenter; when he came by and gave a half-assed proposal, I declined, and the owner freaked out and stripped the place of all the promised appliances. Nevertheless, the building I was looking at would soon be my own ramen shop. That's all that mattered.

Most of her equipment was junk anyway, and in retrospect, starting with an empty space allowed me to build a shop to my specifications. But there was plenty of work ahead of me. There was no lighting to speak of. The counter was a cheap polished pine veneer with curved edges that were beginning to split open like a banana peel. There were no bowls, utensils, or noodle strainers—no stove, oven, or anything that would lead you to believe the space was once a restaurant.

I paced out the cement room, imagining how the kitchen would look. Noodle machine on the far wall, work counter next to it. Dishwasher in the corner, stove next to the noodle machine. In the States, you need an Ansul fire-suppression system set up precisely over the burners, and a duct system with filters, everything perfectly aligned. In my little shop, I had a stainless steel box surrounding a fan in the wall to "direct" smoke outside. The permitting system in Tokyo is a bit more lax than New York's, to say the least. Compared to New York, outfitting a kitchen in Tokyo is a breeze.

The upstairs loft was another story. Judging from the droppings on the floor, the place was infested with rats the size of raccoons. I set about cleaning and gutting the entire thing, then putting in all new floors, walls, and ceilings. I would go to the DIY center, buy truckloads of material, drop it on the floor of the shop, and try to figure out what to do with it.

Just to add a little hiccup to the process, one week after signing the contract and getting the keys, I kicked a basket in a childish fit of frustration. I heard the bones in my big toe crunch, and I cursed in pain. I was in a wheelchair for six weeks. While my crew climbed ladders, painted, ran gas and electric lines, and installed equipment, I sat on the sideline making comments, and doing my crippled best to help. My wife was absolutely furious with me.

Thankfully, I had an enviable team helping me put the shop together. Mari is an acclaimed interior stylist; my brother-in-law Shochan is a set designer and carpenter; and my first hire, Taro, had just graduated from one of the best art schools in Tokyo. I'd met Taro at a party we had at my house. He was interested in learning English and then moving to London, so I said, "Why don't you come work at my ramen shop for a year or two and I'll teach you to speak English?" He agreed; so the three and a half of us built the restaurant together.

I knew that I wanted a bright, modern place, but it had to be unmistakable as a ramen shop. I was a gaijin trying to break into the highly scrutinized, carefully documented, publicly policed world capital of noodle shops. There would be people ready to harp on every missed detail. We ultimately decided to keep the bones of the old shop, but jazzed up the counter with a dark wood-grain laminate, squared off the corners, and added steel trim. We added lighting above and below the bar. Most ramen shops have stools for seating, and generally they're the most uncomfortable stools you can find. Ramen shops are all about fast turnover, and owners don't want customers to feel like they can hang around. But I wanted my business to be focused on service, just like Lutèce had been all those years earlier. I bought nice comfortable stools and decided to worry about shooing customers out the door later.

In New York, dealing with permits, getting community board approval, and finding an honest and reliable contractor are always enormous clusterfucks. In Tokyo, my contractor did everything on a handshake agreement and insisted on not being paid until a month after the shop opened. If there were any problems, he'd fix them without a word. He still comes around regularly to make sure everything's fine. As for my health inspection, a guy came in with a clipboard, and asked if there was a bathroom. There was, and he took a look. He asked if there was a hand sink. There was, which he confirmed, then handed me a form to sign. Done.

I'd lived in Japan for a total of seven years when I decided to open the shop. I didn't see myself as an outsider every second of every day anymore. People in town were accepting from the beginning; they didn't seem to bat an eye. It was a strangely organic process, especially considering that I'd never owned a business before. As I said, I didn't feel a tremendous amount of pressure to succeed. My wife was supportive, and it was just something I really wanted to do. I was tired of sitting at home, talking to my American friends over the Internet. I wanted to use the language and hang out with Japanese people.

I also wanted to make a great bowl of ramen. I worried that people would expect my ramen to suck ass. I wanted to prove them deeply wrong from the outset. At home, I was consumed with researching and perfecting my dashi, sampling flours, cooking pork. I was determined to apply the skills I'd amassed as a cook, and to leave lazy tendencies behind. I'd always had the terrible habit of making great food without recording measurements or taking notes. I heard plenty of stories about new ramen shop owners who thought they'd come up with the perfect recipe at home, only to find themselves lost when they tried to make it in large quantities at the shop.

In my kitchen, I weighed every ingredient in grams and wrote it down. Precision is key to ramen, and crucial to running a restaurant. You have to be able to communicate exactly what you want to the people working for you, and they have to be able to replicate the same results over and over. With experienced cooks, you can just explain the concept and proportions and then count on them to taste things and reproduce your dishes. But when you're selling ramen for seven or eight bucks a bowl, it's impossible to pay veteran cooks twenty bucks an hour. I knew from the outset that I'd be hiring inexperienced helpers, so I'd tried to keep careful measurements and make all my recipes foolproof.

In the midst of all this recipe testing and DIY construction, I never stopped to consider the strangeness of a Jewish guy from Long Island opening a ramen shop in Tokyo. In other words, I was too focused on opening my ramen shop to think about opening my ramen shop.

During my first stint in Japan years earlier, I'd sometimes lapsed into petulance, deliberately acting against the grain out of frustration. Upon my return to the country, I decided from day one that I would try to completely adhere to all cultural nuances. I'd do everything to the letter, try

Right: The Nogamis, who own the tofu shop across the way from Ivan Ramen.
Page 56: Fukuya-san, my butcher. Page 57: Tatsumiya-san, my produce lady.

to make people feel comfortable, and always behave as a Japanese person would. It puts people at ease; it shows that you respect them and their ways. People accept you much more readily and forgive your faux pas more than if your attitude is "I'm gonna do it my way."

So I began putting down roots in the neighborhood. The shop is located in a small corridor of shops, and it was important to me that my business be an extension of the community, so before we even started working on the shop I went to each neighboring shop, introduced myself, and offered a small gift. This is traditional—a properly polite gesture that put me on good footing with everyone.

I was especially interested in the butcher across the way, Fukuya-san. The erratic woman who sold me my shop had told me that the butcher had terrible meat, but it quickly became apparent that this was untrue. In fact,

meeting Fukuya-san was an incredible stroke of luck. I had no idea how to buy meat in bulk in Japan, and lo and behold, a wise, friendly butcher was stationed ten feet away.

I told Fukuya-san that I was excited to work with him and believed strongly in buying locally, but that we needed to work together on price and quality, and he came through. I not only got good prices and high-quality meat, but a leader of the local business association was now my ally. Later, as things began to pick up at the noodle shop, Fukuya-san was an indispensable friend. When more customers began to arrive, I had to make larger and larger quantities of soup, without any way to cool it safely and store it. For months before I could rent more space, Fukuya-san would stay late at his shop every night so that I could bring big stockpots over to his shop. There, he'd hum to himself as he methodically stirred and cooled them for me.

Next on my agenda were vegetables. The local yaoya (vegetable shops) in town varied wildly in quality, and weren't interested in selling in bulk. After visiting nearly every store in the area, I finally found my vegetable connection in the form of a specialty fruit shop near the train station. Tatsumiya-san specialized in produce that was lightly damaged, scraped, or bruised. People in Japan are obsessed with perfect produce—perfectly round, perfectly colored, perfectly smooth fruit and vegetables. And they come at a premium. It's not uncommon for a nice apple to sell for ¥500 (about $6). A small bunch of perfect-looking grapes sell for ¥1,000 to ¥1,500. And then, of course, there are the ¥10,000 melons that have been grown in glass cases to come out as squares. Tatsumiya-san's produce never looked perfect, but it was always delicious and the prices were lower than anywhere else.

In addition to making nice with local vendors, I started building relationships in the broader ramen community. I became friends with Shimamoto-san, the representative from Yamato, the company that sold me my noodle-making machine. When my $15,000, five-hundred-pound noodle machine arrived at the shop three weeks before we were to open, I had no idea how to use it. I'd been making doughs at home on my hand-crank machine, and had a sense of what a good dough should feel like, but this was a new challenge.

Thankfully, Shimamoto-san knows everything there is to know about combining water and flour. He has an entire mental catalogue of flour at his disposal, and knows exactly what percentage of water is necessary to achieve different textures. He has a magical sense with noodles. He talked me through the ways different protein levels of flour interact with each other, how egg whites can add bite, and how to effectively manage the percentage of water to make spectacularly chewy noodles.

Shimamoto-san sent me bags and bags of flour samples. Flour for bread, flour for udon, different kinds of rye flour. At one point, I had twenty bags of flour spread over the counter and laid out on the floor, with notes written in kanji explaining the protein levels and characteristics. I tested combination after combination, making a bowl of ramen with each new dough and trying them on my wife and brother-in-law. They'd say, "Oh god, this noodle is terrible," and I'd go back and make another one.

Whenever I reached an impasse, I'd call up Shimamoto-san and say, "I can't get it right." He'd ask what percentage of water I was using. If I said 36 percent, he'd say, "I really think 38 would be better," or he'd suggest a different flour. Each batch was a little better than the last, and just before opening, I finally figured out how to craft the noodle I wanted.

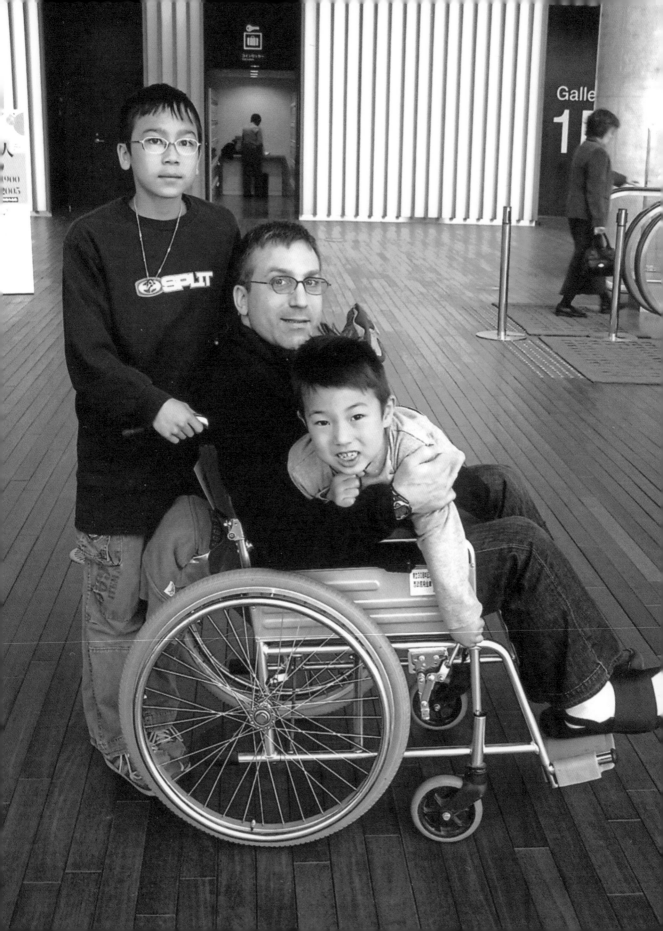

Working with people like Fukuya-san, Tatsumiya-san, and Shimamoto-san was exactly what I had hoped for when I imagined running my own shop. For the first time in my life as a Japanese resident, I was part of a community. My neighbors say I'm more Japanese than Japanese people, which is silly, but I try to embrace as many customs as I can. I became a big proponent of goaisatsu, the proper greetings. Every morning I'd walk around the neighborhood shouting, "Ohayo gozaimasu!" ("Good morning!"), with a bow. I ended up getting a lot of unintended brownie points for this; later on, TV crews would follow me on my morning rounds. But at the time, it was invigorating just to interact with people so full of life, who take their business so seriously and work so hard well into their sixties. I still learn something from them every time we talk.

At Kappabashi, the equivalent of New York's Bowery Street, we bought all of our pots, pans, bowls, chopsticks, and noodle strainers. Kappabashi is heaven on earth for cooks and food nerds. You'll leave every time overloaded with tools you never thought you needed for tasks you never knew you wanted to perform.

We were getting close. The night before our opening, I finally made a bowl of shio ramen that I was really, truly happy with. The interior of the restaurant was set, and Taro made the sign and designed the logo. We chose a font that was reminiscent of a Showa-period coffee shop—a source of nostalgia in Japan—with a little extra flourish. It would be a fitting addition to the funky little shopping arcade where the restaurant was located. Taro ordered stainless steel letters and bought a cheap orange waterproof board. He drilled holes in the board and ran a long length of LED tubing through the holes, then attached the letters and ran stainless steel tubing around the outside of the board.

There's a scene in *Tampopo* where the main character finishes renovating her ramen shop and stands shoulder to shoulder with her companions, looking at the new sign they painted, taking it all in. I had that exact same moment outside my own shop, my chest swelling with pride and validation. We'd built Ivan Ramen ourselves—even if I was confined to a wheelchair for a large part of it.

~~~~~~

Left: Evidence of my continuing dopiness: a week after signing the lease on the shop, I kicked a basket and broke my foot. I was in a wheelchair for most of the restaurant's construction.

The Shop

A week before opening to the public, we planned a series of soft openings for friends and family. Behind the counter, it would just be me and Taro. Taro had no cooking experience and no restaurant aspirations, but he was quick and smart and I figured I could count on him to back me up.

I walked through the kitchen and imagined making each bowl of ramen, where each ingredient was, how I'd move. I grabbed a pen and paper and drew a map, laying out the locations of the utensils, bowls, sauces, noodles, eggs, toppings. Serving ramen is not as complicated as putting out a fine-dining menu, but it's just as easy to screw up, to lose track of what you're doing, leave out a crucial ingredient, let the soup cool down after a lull and not reheat it (the worst ramen infraction is lukewarm soup). All the while, the customers are inches from your face with nothing to do but watch your every move.

A soft opening doesn't give you license to serve lousy food or provide sloppy service, but it removes the pressure of set business hours and menu items; if things get too screwy, you can just shut down. Your friends are the customers, and if you fuck up, they'll understand. For us, the soft openings were a fantastic learning experience—because we got to see exactly how horribly wrong everything would have gone if we'd immediately opened to the public.

We were trying to heat the soup one portion at a time, which bogged down service. We were washing dishes by hand and didn't have a rack to hold the clean ones. At every turn, we'd find something missing or a process we needed to fix. But each night of that week, after serving twenty or thirty people, we'd sit down with a couple of beers and analyze our mistakes. We reconfigured the dish station, decided to keep twenty portions of soup hot at any given time, and learned to move without constantly bumping into one another. Some customers remarked that the shop was a little hard to see from the street, so we installed more signage. We bought a free standing light box and wrote "ラーメンやってるよ" (ramen yateru yo, or roughly, "Hey, we're serving ramen!") in funky Japanese script.

Then Taro designed a poster to put in the window—a list of frequently asked questions that we had heard during the soft opening. Questions like "What does the 'Ivan' in Ivan Ramen mean?" "What kind of ramen do you serve?" "Why did you open a ramen shop?" (Answers: "It's my name, I'm

an American guy from New York," "A double-soup ramen made from rich chicken stock and clean-tasting dashi," and "I saw *Tampopo* in college and it made a big impression on me." Of course, the last answer isn't really the case. I love the movie, but it didn't inspire me to open a ramen shop. The thing is, everyone I spoke to about the shop wanted some kind of explanation for why I'd decided to open it. "*Tampopo* made me do it" was easier to say than "It all began with my year of washing dishes at Tsubo in Syosset, New York . . .").

On June 2, 2007, we opened our doors to the public.

Whenever a new shop opens in Japan, it's traditional for friends, family, and related businesses to send flowers—big garish displays with the name of the sender prominently displayed on a long wooden board sticking out of the vase. It's a way for friends to show support, and for the shop to show that they have the endorsement of prominent community members. The more connected the shop owner is, the more splashy the displays.

Once again, my brother-in-law came to the rescue. He was good friends with Yuko Kotegawa—one of Japan's most famous movie stars—as well as Princess Tenko, the country's most famous magician. On opening day, smack in the middle of our assortment of flowers were two beautiful, ostentatious displays with the names of these beloved entertainers attached. It created a lot of buzz in our little neighborhood. "Who the hell is this gaijin?" they were asking, "and why does he know these celebrities?"

By the time we opened the restaurant, the word *gaijin* had taken on a new meaning to me. I didn't feel so sensitive about it. In general, I think the word's connotations had softened over time, as Japan became a more cosmopolitan country. Really, it all depends on who's saying it and how they're saying it. It can still be hurtful if its utterance is dripping with nastiness. But I knew I was a gaijin opening a ramen shop. That was going to be my hook.

And in fact, it led to our first breakthrough. Shortly before we opened, Mari sent an anonymous tip to one of Japan's preeminent ramen critics, Ohsaki-san, saying that there was a gaijin running a ramen shop in Rokakoen, and his stuff was pretty good. Ohsaki has eaten more than eight thousand bowls of ramen. He's a god among ramen geeks. He is to the Tokyo ramen scene as Will Shortz is to crossword puzzles.

The second or third day we were open, I was behind the counter, still cooking by the seat of my pants. One customer finished his bowl of shio ramen, stood, and started peppering me with questions about my noodles and soup in rapid-fire Japanese. I was in the middle of assembling another

bowl, with chopsticks full of noodles, and I didn't catch the first question. I looked up and said, "Huh?" Rather than repeating the question, he gave me a look that said, "I guess he doesn't understand me," turned on his heels, and walked out the door.

"That was Ohsaki-san," Taro whispered in my ear.

My heart sank. I wondered if I'd just blown it before we'd even really began.

Fortunately, he found my ramen better than my Japanese. In a very brief entry on his blog, he raved about my shio ramen—and with that, I had officially entered the Tokyo ramen scene. There are ten thousand ramen shops in Tokyo, and only a small handful get any kind of media attention, much less words of praise from Ohsaki-san.

After Ohsaki's little review came out, the pace picked up a bit. We'd serve thirty or forty customers each day, rather than ten or fifteen. Ivan Ramen appeared on a few more ramen blogs, and word started to spread. For most of the first summer, though, the shop was still a relatively quiet newcomer.

Being wall-to-wall busy from day one can be as much a curse as a blessing in the restaurant world. There's no time to practice, and no opportunity to

grow on your own terms. Our quiet arrival on the scene meant we didn't have to worry about a line of impatient people stretching down the block.

We were paying our bills, and I was happy to concentrate on making good food and getting through each day. A ramen restaurant doesn't require the same kind of deft, breakneck moves as a fine-dining kitchen. It might be easy to slip into complacency, treating the repetition as monotonous. A lot of people do. But I felt my past chefs sitting on my shoulder. Work clean, prep correctly, label everything, season, taste—those lessons weren't lost on me just because I wasn't working at Lutèce anymore. Even if I wasn't making foie gras torchon, I approached my work with the same commitment to quality. I worked my ass off making forty liters of soup at a time in our hundred-square-foot restaurant. I'd roast tomatoes, braise pork belly, make dashi, and cook sofrito, all in this silly, tiny spot. We were open from 5:30 p.m. to 10:30 p.m., then I'd break down my station, clean up, and start again the next day at 6 a.m.

Any sort of language safety net was gone once the shop opened. I was on my own, precariously negotiating my own contracts, cold-calling new purveyors, and shooting the breeze with customers. My Japanese improved more in those first few months than it had in all my previous years living in Japan. But the day I knew I had really arrived was when one of my suppliers called and casually said they had made a mistake and my katsuobushi (dried bonito) shipment would be a few days late. I spent twenty minutes berating the poor woman on the other end of the phone in fast, fluent, low-class, very angry Japanese. It's a crappy thing to be proud of, but it worked—the shipment arrived four hours later.

I was pretty much a loner in the beginning. Rokakoen is a quiet, isolated area. I was working a shitload of hours, and the only other ramen shop owner I knew personally was the crazy lady I bought the shop from. When Mari was working, the kids slept upstairs in sleeping bags on a fold-out foam couch from IKEA. Isaac was ten and Alex was six when we opened. During the day, they'd hang out with the tofu supplier while he made tofu, or go into the tobacco lady's shop—she'd put cartoons on and give them snacks while their dad was slinging noodles across the way.

Confessions of a Noodle Addict: Ohsaki-San

Ohsaki-san doesn't cut a particularly intimidating figure. He has a round, friendly face, disarming glasses, and a stocky build (although he's nowhere near as portly as you'd expect someone who eats eight hundred bowls of ramen each year to be). But at the time I opened Ivan Ramen, Ohsaki-san was among the most influential, terrifying people who could take a seat at my counter. His word was gospel to ramen devotees. Nobody ate as much ramen as Ohsaki-san, and nobody could make or break a shop as easily as him.

Nowadays, Ohsaki-san has become more of a godfather to the ramen world. He's stopped giving his opinions about individual shops, opting instead to spread the ramen gospel from a neutral throne. He's organized 850 of the 80,000 ramen shops in Japan into a ramen committee that puts on ramen seminars and a five-day ramen event each year. His company, the Ramen Databank, is the most exhaustive resource for ramen hunters in Japan, with a website, magazines, TV shows, and apps.

Ohsaki-san speaks about ramen with the reverence of an obsessive. He's completely serious in his devotion to the stuff. From his earliest experiences with ramen at age eight, he's been addicted to its variety and subtlety. I'd think it was a little bit laughable—if I didn't feel the same way myself.

Ivan Orkin: Why did you start eating ramen, and when did ramen eating become the project that it is for you now?

Ohsaki-san: I was born in Fukushima Prefecture, a place famous for Kitakata ramen. When I was young, I would always eat Kitakata ramen and figured that that was what ramen was.

But then I moved to Tokyo, and found tonkotsu soup and miso soup, and noodles that could be thick or thin. This piqued my curiosity. Each ramen shop had a different style, so I just started eating. If you ask a mountain climber why he climbs mountains, he'll say, "The mountain was there." I decided to eat ramen because there was a ramen shop in front of me.

IO: What's your mountain? What's the goal of eating so much ramen?

O: My purpose is to try every ramen shop. But every month sixty new ramen shops open in Tokyo alone. Each new ramen shop has a new style and a new type of ramen, and I want to eat everything. It's an endless goal, endless eating. This year beef ramen appeared. Last year, there was none. Ten years ago, there was no cold ramen.

Ramen history only started a hundred years ago. If sushi is an adult, then one-hundred-year-old ramen is just a child, a junior-high-school student. If it studies and grows, it will become an adult.

IO: Where does ramen exist in the pantheon of Japanese cuisine?

O: I don't think of ramen as Japanese cuisine. Ramen has become a world cuisine. Ramen is popular in New York, in France, in Germany. Everybody knows sushi as sushi. Until recently, everybody thought of ramen as just noodles. Now people can distinguish ramen as ramen, and like sushi, it is its own unique cuisine.

IO: Can you explain the idea of kodawari?

O: A long time ago, we only had imported American cars. Then we began to look closely and change small things, developing something new. The same thing began in ramen in 1996.

IO: Why 1996? Was there an event that changed things?

O: There was. The Internet started. Customers began putting images of ramen on the Internet. Before that, a ramen maker could visit different ramen shops and just steal their techniques. After 1996, you could see if one ramen shop was a copy of another. Ramen shops had to start developing original styles.

Ramen history is one hundred years old now. For ninety years, it was the same, but since 1996, the number of types of ramen has doubled. The difference before and after 1996 is like BC and AD.

IO: Is that when you began seriously eating ramen?

O: I began eating ramen forty-five years ago. I'm fifty-three years old now. When I was young, I'd eat two hundred or three hundred bowls of ramen in one year—a very slow pace. But after the Internet, after 1996, I could get more information about new shops. Now I eat around eight hundred bowls each year.

IO: Jesus—do you eat anything else?

O: I love Italian and French food. But even after eating a full meal, I can still eat three bowls of ramen. I used to go to ramen shops and I'd eat a rice bowl on the side, but now I just stick to the ramen. The first time I came to Ivan Ramen I ate two bowls: the shio and the shoyu.

IO: What was your first impression of Ivan Ramen? Be honest.

O: Ramen is a very sensitive food, and I had never seen a foreigner make delicious ramen. As I walked here from the train station, I thought maybe I'd find something simple, but not delicious. I was skeptical. When I arrived, I saw the kitchen and what you were doing. I saw that you were warming up the chashu before serving it; the chashu is usually just sliced and then placed cold on the ramen. That was the first thing that impressed me.

Even Japanese ramen makers don't make their own noodles, but you make everything—noodles, soup, chashu, everything. When I ate the ramen, I realized it was not a halfway bowl, it was perfect. I saw that ramen's history had changed here. You were a chef before; your skill as a chef improved the ramen. Sometimes an Italian chef or a French chef may open a ramen shop, but they'll make Western-style ramen. You still have traces of a Western style, but your ramen really is Japanese.

IO: How often do you go into a shop and see something new, something that changes the history of ramen?

O: Twenty or thirty percent show me something new. But each time I come to Ivan Ramen, I don't see the same thing as other ramen shops.

IO: Do you generally revisit ramen shops?

O: There are two types of ramen junkies: the repeater and the collector. I'm a collector—I try to eat as many different bowls as I can. There are probably many hundreds of people who eat five hundred bowls of ramen in a year. Then there's those who have maybe one bowl a day—there are probably about five thousand of those people in Japan. I eat about eight hundred bowls each year.

IO: What is your idea of a perfect bowl of ramen?

O: I've never met the perfect bowl of ramen. In general, I like shoyu ramen, because it reminds me of the ramen I ate when I was a child—it's nostalgic ramen.

IO: Is there an objective model—should the noodles be one way and the soup one way?

O: I can't say that the noodles or soup should be one way or another. If that were the case, ramen would stop evolving. I want ramen to keep improving. Sushi and soba are very traditional, so it's hard to introduce a new style. Ramen can change. Plus, not everyone can afford to eat expensive sushi at places like Jiro. Rich, poor—everyone can eat ramen.

The Absurdity

The big break came at the end of August, two months after we opened.

In Japan, a huge percentage of the shows on TV are variety shows. Each one comprises different segments and sketches, including at least one about food. All these shows, from the most popular to the little public-access types, have armies of assistant directors, who are paid next to nothing to comb the Web for stories. As my name and story started to get out onto the blogs, I must have popped up on the radars of a few ADs. I was invited to appear on one of the big prime-time variety shows.

It was a show that celebrated different cuisines, hosted by this famous comedy duo called London Boots—like the Japanese Martin and Lewis. It would feature a panel of comedians and famous ramen makers who would taste and comment on my food. In spite of the heavy comedy angle, the show was considered a relatively serious affair, and being on it meant a big boost to any restaurant.

I was determined not to get caught with my pants down. I'd worked at Mesa Grill when it was written up in the *New York Times*; Bobby Flay told us to get ready, because we were about to get our asses kicked. Popularity is a double-edged sword, and it's easy to get overwhelmed and start serving cold food and running out of product. I hired another part-timer to help out, and made sure we had double every ingredient—the minute I reached for some sliced pork and there wasn't any, we'd be finished. No matter how popular you or your restaurant become, you want the food to shine brightest. You want your peers to come in and eat the food and think, "Yes, he deserved the praise."

The show was broadcast on a Sunday night. They showed a little segment about my life and the shop, and I bantered with the comedians for a while. They ate my ramen with gusto, and lavished praise on it. It was ludicrous, watching myself on Japanese TV, but the most ludicrous thing was that on Monday, there was a line of thirty people waiting outside half an hour before we opened. It kept up every day, without fail. On several occasions, people waited outside in the middle of a typhoon. We hunkered down, focused, and banged out the best food we could, trying not to become one of the many restaurants that have imploded under the weight of media attention.

My parents came in for the first time a month or two after the show aired. There was a line of twenty people outside, and I insisted that they wait with everyone else. It makes me sound like a horrible son, but here were all these good people who had schlepped out to my shop, just to stand in a heinous line. I couldn't bring myself to whisk my parents past them, like a pair of VIPs at a nightclub. But my parents are good sports—they thought it was fun to get the full experience.

As fate would have it, while they stood in line, they started chatting up an English-speaking man who just happened to be a well-regarded Japanese writer and book editor. By the end of their meal, my parents had basically talked the guy into giving me a deal for a Japanese-language cookbook. Books are churned out much more indiscriminately and with more regularity in Japan, but still, the book would add to the shop's legend.

The lines kept growing. People were waiting two hours for a bowl of noodles. It felt a little perverse—two hours for a fifteen- or twenty-minute experience. But I wasn't complaining.

Following the crowds came the blog entries. My early favorite read: "I thought for sure the soup would have a ketchup flavor to it, so I was surprised and thrilled to eat such an authentic, delicious bowl of ramen. Sorry, Ivan, for thinking such negative things about you."

Right: On the right is Gyaru Sone, a TV personality whose claim to fame was the astounding amount she could eat. She was visiting the shop for a game show where she competed against three other guys to see who could eat the most ramen. Nine bowls later, she won handily.

Every news article, blog post, TV interview, and conversation focused on the gaijin angle. Every positive review started, "I expected Ivan Ramen to be terrible, but . . ." The online forums were alive with conspiracy theories. Some people said I was a front for a large Korean corporation; others claimed that I was just a front for a Japanese chef; my favorite one speculated that I was really Japanese and was just pretending to be a foreigner.

One night, just before we opened the shop, amidst all the uncertainty and toil, I felt a sudden upsurge of positivity. I looked my wife in the eye and told her that I would have one of the hottest restaurants in Tokyo and that my ramen would be one of the best bowls in the city. She said, "Yeah, sure. That's cute." I was being a little facetious, but I was also confident in my ability. I don't think Mari was a full believer until April 2008.

April was the month that Minoru Sano, aka Sano-san, aka the Ramen Devil, came to Ivan Ramen to film his show. Again, Sano-san was a pioneer of the kodawari movement; he'd elevated ramen to a craft on par with sushi. He was a larger-than-life personality, a television star, and a terror. He'd brought stronger men than me to tears.

Now he would sit in my ramen shop and pass judgment on my food for millions of television viewers. He came with a half-dozen cameras and two members of a popular boy band. He was dressed in his standard all-white, perfectly pressed cooking uniform—like the ones sushi chefs wear—with his hair slicked back.

Like every other show I'd appeared on in the past year, this one began with my visitors passing through the doorway and being shocked by the sight of a white face behind the counter. I waved my hand and gave a goofy "hello." They peppered me with standard questions about my motivation for opening a shop and the particulars of my ramen. Then it was time to put up or shut up. I made three bowls of shio ramen and handed them over the counter into their waiting hands.

The show wasn't *Ramen Oni*, the one where Sano-san would walk into failing restaurants and scream at the proprietors about their inadequacies. This was more of a travel show, where he'd visit shops and taste the ramen and that was that. He suggested that I increase the water content of my noodles by 1 percent, which I did, and which did improve them. That show,

and Sano-san's quiet nod of approval, elevated my status to one of the pre-mier ramen cooks in Tokyo.

After Sano-san's visit, things were bananas. For two years straight, we had lines around the block every day. I was a frequent curiosity on TV. It became almost routine. Because I'd made the mistake of stating on the FAQ poster in front of the shop that *Tampopo* is my favorite movie, every inter-viewer in Japan began by suggesting—insisting, really—that the movie had hypnotized me into a bizarre quest to open my own ramen shop. Then, at the end of most shows, the host would ask me to write a word or phrase in kanji that expressed my feelings about ramen. With a Sharpie, I would scrawl "I am the spirit of ramen" or some horrible crap like that on a large white poster. It was all silly, but I took it in stride, because, hell, I was hav-ing a good time and every show meant a bump for the shop.

When I'd made my prediction to Mari about Ivan Ramen being one of the biggest shops in Tokyo, I'd also told her that we'd have our own instant ramen within a year. She'd laughed at that, too. In 2008, very few people had their own branded instant ramen. Essentially, I was like a garage band singer telling his girlfriend that he was going to play Madison Square Gar-den after his first guitar lesson.

Then the Garden called. Sapporo Ichiban, Japan's third largest instant-ramen maker, called me to say they were looking to manufacture and sell Ivan Ramen brand shio ramen. I actually hate instant and fast food; I'd eaten cup ramen only once ever in the States. But I couldn't resist the siren call of my own smiling mug on the package.

The first time the R&D guys from Sapporo Ichiban visited, they came with a sample ready for me to try. They had surreptitiously eaten at Ivan Ramen a few times during the past month and had concocted an approxi-mation that they thought was a winner. It wasn't. The noodles tasted of plastic, and the soup had a bizarre chemical aftertaste. I made them prom-ise not to release any product until I gave my approval. No sane person would expect an instant ramen to taste exactly like the ramen you get at the shop, but I wasn't going to be satisfied until we got as close as we could. I thought of instant-ramen shoppers as visitors to my store—if they couldn't make it in to the shop, they deserved a decent approximation.

We went back and forth eight times. The R&D guys would bring their samples, and I'd supply a thermos of boiling water, and we'd scatter little packets of fat, seasoning, and dried chashu all over the counter. We'd cook the ramen and taste it and I'd offer notes. I'd make them bowls of the real shio ramen so they could get a clear idea of what we were aiming for. Each

round improved a little from the last. The aftertaste disappeared. Sapporo Ichiban agreed to add whole wheat to the noodles, something they'd never done before. By the time I gave my final okay, it tasted good—not the real thing, but something I could comfortably put my name upon.

When it hit the store shelves, it was the fastest-selling instant ramen the company had ever produced—three hundred thousand units in less than a month. I honestly believe it was the work we put into the product and not my budding celebrity that did it. There's a high bar for instant and fast food in Japan, and I think we produced a more than decent bowl of instant ramen.

On New Year's Day 2009, I sat back and assessed what the past year had brought. I was the proprietor of an obscenely busy ramen shop, a cookbook author, the face of an instant ramen brand, and soon-to-be father of three—Mari was expecting our son Ren in March.

For the majority of Japanese people, New Year's Day is spent glued to the TV. Nobody goes out. Nothing's open. At two o'clock in the afternoon, January 1, 2009, Ivan Ramen would hit its peak. A major network broadcast an eighteen-minute documentary on our shop as one of the best restaurants in Tokyo, followed by a live segment with me serving ramen to celebrities. When we reopened after the year-end break, we had lines from the minute we opened until the minute we closed. Customers would bang on the shuttered doors trying to get in even after we turned out the lights. I began taking one of my business cards, scribbling "I'm last" on it, and handing it to the last person we could serve before we ran out of food. I bestowed upon them the undignified job of delivering the bad news to any further visitors.

It felt good to be popular, to meet and interact with so many people on a daily basis. It's what I'd wanted—to feel like a genuine part of the community. But I was still mostly a loner in the ramen community. I'd made my rounds and tried to ingratiate myself with the bigwigs, but mostly I kept my head down trying to keep up with the shop. Talk to any big-name chef: no matter how famous they get or how busy their restaurants are, all they really want is the respect of their peers.

That's why my favorite moment of the year occurred before the big New Year's show, and it happened in someone else's restaurant. Every company

Pages 80 to 81: When you open a restaurant in Japan, people send flowers. You display them to show how popular you are and how excited people are for your restaurant. This was the floral display and line of people waiting for the opening of my second restaurant, Ivan Ramen Plus.

and profession in Japan has a year-end party called a bonenkai. (The end of one year and the beginning of the next is an important and spiritual time in Japan.) When I received an invitation to take part in a bonenkai with the ramen elite, I nearly wept. To be included in their group—this meant the world to me.

Walking into the cavernous restaurant where the party was being held, I was a bit overwhelmed. The main floor of the restaurant was like a big izakaya, filled mostly with young guys dressed in jeans, T-shirts, and beanies and with a few days' growth of scruffy beard. Then, up a little ring of stairs, tucked in the back, were all the old dons of ramen—Maijima-san from Setagaya, Koitani-san from Jiraigen, Morizumi-san from Chabuya—leaning back and chuckling at the youngsters. I stood in the middle of it all, wondering what the hell I was doing there.

But in swooped the owner from Kiraboshi—a well-regarded tonkotsu shop in western Tokyo—to save the day. He took me under his wing and began introducing me around the room. A lot of these guys were my heroes—I'd eaten at their shops, looked longingly into their kitchens, and wondered if I could ever make ramen as good as theirs. These guys had fed me and inspired me without knowing it.

Someone handed me a beer. Before I finished that one, another was thrust into my hands. The details of the night after this point are lost in a haze of drunken camaraderie. After all my struggles just to fit in, here I was being schmoozed and boozed by my peers. I wasn't just a white guy with a ramen shop in Tokyo, wondering if anyone would ever come. I'd made it.

Epilogue

In 2010, we opened our second restaurant, Ivan Ramen Plus. I had three kids at home and things were going strong at Ivan Ramen, but I figured I ought to stay ambitious, lest I settle into complacency and mediocrity.

The second restaurant would be a little more progressive design-wise, and a little more edgy as far as the menu was concerned. My mother-in-law chose the location again, and again I got an out-of-the-way suburb with no foot traffic. I took out a zero-interest business loan from the city and again built the place myself. Our first day we served 420 diners—in a sixteen-seat restaurant. Both restaurants were running at full capacity with no signs of slowing down.

Then came the earthquake.

On March 3, 2011, Alex, Ren, Mari, and I were in the car on our way to school for the parent-teacher conference day. We were stopped at a light when suddenly the road started undulating. The asphalt was moving like liquid; cars were bouncing up and down for a solid three or four minutes. In the other earthquakes I've experienced, by the time you realize you're in an earthquake, it's already over. This one went on and on.

Left: Mari and me in Tokyo.

When it finally stopped, we headed straight to the school. Everybody was already outside on the ball field. We found Isaac right away and sat there with him through a major aftershock, then waited until the teachers gave us the okay to leave. We drove home immediately, narrowly missing the traffic that blocked other people for hours on end. At home, just a few things were shattered here and there—nothing compared to what other parts of the country were experiencing. Over the next few hours and days, stories began trickling in over the Internet—horrible accounts of mothers separated from their children by overwhelming tsunamis—then the news of the nuclear reactor melting down. There were massive aftershocks each day for the next week.

Mari's parents left for Osaka, but we decided to stay. We were scared, but I didn't feel right leaving my staff in the middle of a crisis. I couldn't look them in the eye and say, "Look, we're gonna leave Tokyo for a while—take care of the store."

I was in New York during 9/11, and the feeling was eerily similar. Everyone in New York was scared. But your average person can't up and move just because they're scared. People's lives are tied to their cities. It's the same way in Tokyo. The Japanese are a strong, resilient people. I'm proud of both of my cities—their stories of courage and sacrifice are equally indelible in my mind.

We ended up leaving Tokyo nine months after the earthquake, moving back to New York. I count us as lucky: we have another place to go, with family and resources. Not everyone does. I tried to do my part raising money and making ramen for the displaced for the nine months we held on, starting the night of the earthquake, when we were packed with people who were walking home past the restaurant. We served as many as we could.

Things are calmer these days. When I come to Tokyo, I look around sometimes and it almost seems like nothing happened. Everyone's eating whatever they feel like without fear of radiation or pollution. They're traveling wherever they feel like going, doing whatever they feel like doing.

But the economic impact of the earthquake is undeniable—hundreds of billions of dollars of damage. Infrastructure was destroyed around the country. Whole rice fields were filled with saltwater and will never grow rice again. Many of the towns that were destroyed were already struggling—fishing villages and farming communities.

But our restaurants in Tokyo are picking up again. Kyodo, the town where Ivan Ramen Plus is located, has turned out to be a little more challenging than I thought it would be, but we've got our regulars and our ratings on the Internet get better and better. Trying to sell a refined version of a simple food is a challenging proposition anywhere in the world.

And being the hardheaded man that I am, I decided to try it again—this time in New York. As I write this, I'm in the process of building a ramen shop in Manhattan. Sure, there's lots of ramen in America already, but I'll just say it: it's still nowhere near the level of what we've got in Tokyo. My chef friends tell me that New Yorkers will refuse to eat their soup as hot as I want them to, or that my customers will want to linger over cocktails and appetizers rather than messily slurp down a bowl of noodles and hit the road. They're probably right, but hey, I'm an American and I fell in love with ramen the way it was meant to be eaten. There are undoubtedly more people like me out there.

I feel torn about leaving Japan. On the one hand, coming back to America has opened up new opportunities for Ivan Ramen. But there was so much more work to be done in Tokyo, too. Japan was my first love and I can't shake the sense that I let her down. Whenever I'm back to visit, every six weeks or so, I'm overcome with a feeling of being home. But my kids are adjusted to American life now (Ren is losing his Japanese skills at an alarming rate), and the prospect of moving back to Tokyo seems distant at best.

I'm more of an outsider in New York than I was in Tokyo, a gaijin in my own country. I've never opened a restaurant in America, and the layers of bureaucracy are mind-boggling. I think like a Japanese person. I wait to get my hair cut until I'm back in Rokakoen, so I can have the guy three doors down from Ivan Ramen do it the way I like it. When I visit Tokyo, my wife and kids send me with a laundry list of things I've got to bring back—specific pencils and pens, pickled seaweed, plum wine.

Before we moved to Tokyo together, Mari had warned me that I'd most likely never live in New York again. Once we left America and settled into a new life, I'd be too old to up and do it again. Imagine what that would be like!

Imagine starting over yet again.

Ivan Ramen's Shio Ramen

A diner walks in from the cold and puts his money into the ordering machine. He punches the button for shio ramen, and the machine spits out his ticket. He grabs a seat, and places his ticket on the counter. I give him a smile, say hello, and set to work.

I grab a bowl and saucer from the shelf. The bowl is stark white and sloped on one side. It's not exactly traditional, but it looks and feels like a bowl that's meant to hold noodles. In front of me are square stainless steel containers filled with shio tare (salty seasoning), chicken and pork fat, katsuobushi (shaved dried bonito) powder, menma (bamboo shoots), negi (shredded Japanese green onions), chashu (pork), and soft-boiled eggs. Ladles jut out from the containers, each one sized to deliver the exact amount needed of each ingredient.

On the burner is a roasting pan holding a thin soup in which I'll warm slices of pork. Next to that is a large stainless steel pot with simmering chicken soup and dashi; in the rear is an extra gallon of soup waiting to replenish the stainless steel pot. Next to the range is the yudemenki, or noodle cooker, which is set for a low boil. A few wooden handles are barely visible through plumes of rising steam. On a wire rack next to the cooker are lidded rectangular aluminum containers holding coils of fresh noodles.

The first things that go into the bowl are the building blocks of flavor: thirty grams of shio tare, ten grams each of freshly rendered chicken and pork fat, then smoky fish powder and salt. I peel back the lid from the container of noodles, and the aroma of fresh wheat rises into the humid air (the shop is small and perpetually steeped in noodle steam). I set a timer— even after all these bowls, I still time every order—and slip the noodles into the boiling water.

Fifty seconds to go. Chashu goes into the roasting pan. I dip a large ladle into the soup and pour it over the seasoning components. As the soup swirls into the bowl, the fat melts and glistens, and the fish powder rises in dots to the top of the liquid. The moment the timer goes off, I lift the basket of noodles from the boiler and vigorously shake it, sending drops of boiling water flying. Then, using long wooden chopsticks, I lay the noodles into the bowl, lifting and folding them over themselves to separate and evenly distribute them.

To finish, I slice an egg with a piece of fishing line tautly rigged across two pushpins, then gingerly separate it and place the two halves on top of the waiting soup. Cured bamboo shoots go next, before I pluck the chashu from its bath and lay it across the top of the noodles. To finish, a mound of bright white threads of negi.

I wipe errant splashes of soup from the side of the bowl, set a renge spoon on the saucer, and swivel the dish so that the egg is facing the customer. I wait for eye contact, then I stretch out my arms, bowl held aloft, as the customer's hands stretch out to meet mine.

There goes another bowl of Ivan ramen.

When I told Enamoto-san, the manager at Ivan Ramen, that I was going to include the entire, unaltered recipe for our shio ramen in this book, he was incredulous.

"You really should reconsider," he said with the tone of a disappointed dad.

His reaction stems from this idea among ramen shop owners that you take your recipe with you to the grave. It's not a completely foreign idea to Americans. We always hear about the guys with secret barbecue sauce or pizza dough recipes that they guard like leprechauns hoarding their treasure. If you ask a ramen chef about his methods or his recipes, the room generally gets really quiet, and Japanese ramen cookbooks are always maddeningly vague in how they list ingredients or describe their processes.

When I started thinking seriously about making ramen, I would visit other people's shops hoping to pick the chefs' brains. I'd be sitting at the bar, inching closer and closer to the action, pumping myself up to ask a question. But at the last second, I'd always lose courage. I had a distinct vision in my head of the guy opening his eyes wide with rage, then assaulting me with a spoon.

One day I said to Shimazaki-san—one of my close friends and proprietor of one of the most serious and respected ramen shops in all of Tokyo—"Man, none of these ramen chefs want to share anything with me." He looked at me and laughed, "That's because they don't know anything. They learn how to make ramen from their master, and they can't veer from that recipe."

There's probably some truth to what he said, but whatever the reason, when it came to making my own bowl of ramen, I was on my own. To be frank, I didn't really sweat it. I considered the flavors I like, the style of food I like, and I made a bowl of ramen to match.

I like clean, sharp, refined flavors. My ramen is sophisticated and complex in the way it's built—smoked fish and pork and chicken make multiple appearances in different forms—but I don't think it has to taste that way. For me, a perfect bowl of ramen is balanced—not too salty, not too fatty. The soup sparkles with the taste of its ingredients. If it's a fish soup, you can taste the fish. If it's chicken, you taste chicken.

But there's no one formula for great ramen; that's why it's so fucking hard. Sometimes you want a light, bright soup to complement really delicate noodles. But certain noodles require more fat to ensure that the soup will stick to the noodle. Shimazaki-san uses chicken fat from specific chickens from Akita prefecture, and it's the most delicious thing. But it's only in the past ten or fifteen years that ramen chefs have really begun to think of their ramen with this single-mindedness (and even now, only 10 or 20 percent of us are making artisanal or kodawari ramen), though that focus and attention to detail has been a hallmark of other Japanese cuisines forever.

Take something like tempura. In the States, we order tempura in combination platters—sweet potato, carrot, broccoli, onion, two pieces of shrimp. I don't think there are any restaurants in America specializing solely in tempura. But go to a good tempura shop in Tokyo and all you'll get is tempura. And when it's done right, tempura is the absolute pinnacle of the frying arts. A good shop will switch out their oil every twenty minutes. They cook one piece at a time. The chef will put one little piece of shrimp or asparagus in front of you and tell you to eat it with a little sprinkle of this salt or that sauce. The menu is entirely dependent on the season. Certain times of the year, you'll get mountain vegetables, other times it'll be aromatic grasses and flower buds. Some things are only available for a week, or even a day. You eat one item at a time and you just rejoice in the flavor of that vegetable.

I don't say this to disparage American culture, or to say that Americans don't understand this way of eating, or couldn't go that far themselves. But we tend to like choices, and I don't think we've fully been introduced to this idea of just sticking to one thing, and learning to appreciate that one thing for what it is. Americans have begun to understand sushi that way. What I am trying to do—along with other kodawari ramen makers—is elevate ramen to that same level.

My fervent hope is to get Americans to enjoy ramen as a dish, along with all the rituals that surround it. Ramen must be eaten quickly, while it's very hot. Ice cream doesn't taste good if you wait till it's dripping down your arm onto your pants. Brick-oven pizza doesn't taste good after you drive it home and plop down in front of the TV and take a big soggy bite. Ramen's the same way. You have to eat it while the fat is still smoking hot and the noodles are still chewy. You take a big airy slurp so that all the flavors come together as they enter your mouth. You get into a rhythm, and then, oh my god, it's fucking gone. I always laugh when a cute girl wearing Chanel walks in and absolutely goes to town on a bowl of ramen. There's fat splashing all

over her fancy shirt and her face is glistening with beads of fat and sweat. She's just like, "Fuck it, I'm eating ramen."

So this book includes the entire recipe for Ivan Ramen shio ramen, exactly as it's made at the shop in Rokakoen. Shio ramen is the first ramen I ever made, and it's the gold standard at my restaurants. It's intimidating only in the sense that it's time consuming to source all the ingredients and prepare the slowly simmered components. I designed the recipes with the idea that noncooks would be executing them at the shop. (There aren't too many cooking-academy grads knocking down my door looking for work.) This means that anyone with a few basic cooking skills and a lot of patience can replicate my shops' ramen.

The inhumanely ambitious can try to make a bowl in one all-day marathon (you'd better get up early). The slightly less crazy will try it over the course of several days or a week. But the majority of you will start by making one or two components, buying the rest from the store. I recommend you start this way and work your way up to the balls-out approach. Sometimes I forget about how arduous a task it is to build a bowl of ramen from scratch. In Tokyo, I can just pop into the shop and hit the guys up for some noodles, shio tare, menma, or braised pork.

Since I've begun planning my restaurant in New York, I've been making ramen from scratch in my home kitchen again. It hasn't gotten any easier, but I'd nearly forgotten the rewards that come with it. It's like putting together a puzzle. You have all these pieces spread out across the counter, and you have no idea how the whole thing will come together. Finally, you step back and see that you've got this beautiful bowl of noodles. Every time I make a bowl of homemade ramen, I fall in love with it again—both the process and the dish. It's the epitome of slow food.

To keep the process as straightforward and appealing as possible, I've ordered the recipes as follows:

First are the instructions for assembling a bowl of Ivan Ramen shio ramen once you've got all the components lined up in front of you.

Then come recipes for each individual component—chicken fat and pork fat, tare, katsuobushi salt, double soup, noodles, and so on.

After that, I've included a few alternate-use recipes—nonramen ways for you to make use of the individual components. These are dishes I've served at the restaurant, or staples I've made over and over again for my family at home. Please experiment on your own. All of the individual ramen components are very versatile. Don't get too caught up in this being a ramen cookbook. Make the chicken fat—make a liter of it. Put some in the freezer, and the next time you make chicken pot pie, use chicken fat in the crust and chicken fat to sauté the vegetables.

After the shio ramen section are recipes for a few other ramen variations we serve at the restaurant. These are just as true to what we serve in the shop as the shio ramen recipe. Some of them are equally daunting, but they also share many components with the shio ramen.

Finally, there are a few side dishes and a couple of ice creams we also serve at the restaurants. If you're going to spend morning to evening making a bowl of ramen that your friends and family will slurp down in five minutes, you ought to consider serving some of these as appetizers and dessert. Don't treat yourself like a ramen shop owner! Draw the meal out a bit with beers and sake and shochu. Make a whole Japanese evening out of it.

A caveat: no matter how you approach the recipes in this book, accept that the quality of ingredients and equipment available to you will depend on where you live. You can get katsuobushi in California or New York or Iowa, but you probably won't find the exact same custom-milled aromatic flours that I use in Tokyo. My dream is that you'll read these recipes, get the outline in your head, consider your own tastes, and say, "I'm willing to fall on my face, but I'm going to try to make a great bowl with what's available to me." Finally, BUY A METRIC SCALE AND LIQUID MEASURE. I'm including both measurements, but frankly metric is more accurate.

Maybe your first bowl won't be exactly what you get at my shop, but I'm pretty confident it'll be better than anything else you've ever had.

Shio Ramen

THE COMPLETE BOWL

Let's say you've got all your ramen components prepped and ready, lined up on the counter. The chashu's warm. The soup's simmering on the stove. Appropriate ladles are matched to their respective sauces. From here, assembling a bowl of ramen is a cinch. (I know, I know, you've spent a week sourcing ingredients, boiling chickens, rendering fat, and braising chashu. Now you know how I feel—so when you come in to the restaurant, eat your soup while it's boiling hot like I asked you to!)

It should be obvious, but I'll say it anyway: have everything ready before you start assembling. You shouldn't be flipping to page X halfway through a bowl of ramen. Recipes for each individual component appear in the pages following this recipe. Tackle them one at a time, then return here when you're ready to assemble a complete bowl.

Makes 1 bowl

10 milliliters (2 teaspoons) warm CHICKEN FAT (page 104)

10 milliliters (2 teaspoons) warm PORK FAT (page 105)

30 milliliters (2 tablespoons) room-temperature SHIO TARE (page 107)

5 grams (1 tablespoon) KATSUOBUSHI SALT (page 111)

1 Bring a pot of unsalted water to a boil for the noodles.

2 In the bottom of a ramen bowl, combine the chicken fat, pork fat, shio tare, and katsuobushi salt.

3 Keep the double soup simmering in a covered saucepan over low heat, but make sure it doesn't reduce.

4 Drop the noodles into the boiling water and cook until just barely al dente. The noodles at Ivan Ramen take exactly 50 seconds to cook, but yours will almost certainly differ. Experiment with a few threads and see how long they take. Just before the noodles are ready, ladle the simmering double soup into the bowl. **(CONTINUED)**

270 milliliters (1 cup) DOUBLE SOUP (page 113), simmering

130 grams (4½ ounces) TOASTED RYE NOODLES (page 119)

2 pieces MENMA (page 123)

1 thick slice PORK BELLY CHASHU (page 127), warmed in its cooking liquid or in the noodle water as it comes to a simmer

1 room-temperature HALF-COOKED EGG (page 131)

Finely shredded green onions or negi (Japanese green onions), for garnish

(CONTINUED)

5 Drain the noodles thoroughly, shaking them well in the strainer to remove as much water as possible, then lay them in the bowl. Lift them with a pair of chopsticks and fold them back over themselves so that they don't clump into a ball.

6 Float the two pieces of menma in the soup. Place the chashu in the center of the bowl.

7 Slice the egg in half. (This is best accomplished with a taut piece of nylon fishing line. The egg yolk won't stick, and you'll end up with a perfect cut). Place the egg halves next to the chashu.

8 Pile the green onions in the center of the bowl. Serve or start eating as soon as possible.

Fat

SHIO RAMEN COMPONENT 1

Of all the ingredients that make ramen ramen, fat is the one that can't be replaced or omitted. This is especially difficult for Western cooks to grasp, and judging from the many bowls I've eaten in the States, this is where American ramen cooks tend to miss the mark. In Western kitchens, we're taught to painstakingly remove the fat from our stocks and soups, but in Japan, we painstakingly add it. At Ivan Ramen, I use different combinations of vegetable, chicken, and pork fat, although it's most common to use only pork fat.

Fat is what gives ramen its mouthfeel, body, and a lot of umami. It's what causes the soup to stick to the noodles. And if the soup doesn't stick to the noodles, you've got nothing. Visit a tonkotsu ramen shop, and you'll find a thick slick of pork fat floating on top of the soup. By the time you finish eating, your lips will be sticky with the stuff. That's more fat than I like in my ramen (and the older I get, the less I'm able to handle gut bombs like that), but you really can't overestimate the importance of fat, even in a light soup.

The quality of the fat is always going to depend on the quality of the animal. I go out of my way to find good free-range chickens and humanely raised pork here in the States. Fat made from industrial animals can have a certain off smell to it. What you get from good animals just tastes cleaner, and more like pork or chicken.

(CONTINUED)

CHICKEN FAT

So here's this Jewish guy from New York making ramen in Tokyo. If you're Jewish, you notice that he's slathering everything with schmaltz, and you laugh a little. They don't call chicken fat "schmaltz" in Japan, but that's what it is. Along with the rye noodles I make, it's one of two little nods to my upbringing. No one in Tokyo gives a rat's ass, but it pleases me to step back and see that some of the flavors and ingredients that I grew up with have become part of my food ten thousand miles away and decades later. The schmaltz is the first thing that goes into every bowl of shio ramen I serve.

Makes about 235 milliliters (1 cup)

450 grams (1 pound) chicken fat (or skin and trimmings, if you can't find fat), chopped

1 Place the chicken fat in a heavy-bottomed saucepan or pot and cover with 2.5 centimeters (1 inch) of water. Bring to a boil, then turn the heat down to low to maintain a very gentle simmer.

2 Simmer gently, uncovered, until the fat has rendered and all that's left is some shriveled meat or skin. This might take as long as 3 hours; add more water as necessary to keep the skin or fat covered.

3 Strain the liquid through a fine-mesh strainer and discard the solids. Refrigerate the liquid overnight.

4 The next day, remove the solidified fat and discard the liquid.

5 Melt the fat in a saucepan over low heat, then pour into a container. Store covered in the refrigerator for a week. (Alternatively, you can slice the solidified fat into small chunks and store in the freezer for 3 months.)

PORK FAT

In Japan, you can buy beautiful slabs of back fat for rendering; it's a little harder to find the same in the States. Lately I've been asking my butcher for fat trimmings, which are dirt cheap and still yield a pretty flavorful fat.

Makes about
700 milliliters (3 cups)

450 grams (1 pound) pork fat back or trimmings

1 Cut the fat into square chunks measuring about 5 centimeters (2 inches) and place them in a heavy-bottomed saucepan or pot. Cover with 2.5 centimeters (1 inch) of water and bring to boil, then turn the heat down to medium to maintain a simmer.

2 Simmer gently, uncovered, until the fat is rendered into a layer of melted fat and the solids are very soft and tender—about 3 hours. Add more water as necessary to keep the pot from drying out.

3 Strain the liquid through a fine-mesh strainer. Refrigerate the liquid and softened chunks of fat separately overnight.

4 The next day, skim the layer of fat from the reserved cooking liquid and add to a saucepan along with the chunks of softened fat. Cook over medium heat until the skimmed fat has melted back into a liquid. Puree the mixture in a food processor until smooth.

5 Cool to room temperature, then store in an airtight container in the refrigerator for a week, or in the freezer for 3 months.

Shio Tare

SHIO RAMEN COMPONENT 2

Shio tare is the seasoning in shio ramen—the component that gives the ramen its saltiness. And even though shio ramen translates as "salt ramen," it shouldn't be overly salty. Made properly, it should give the dish the depth of flavor that good salt can provide, without overseasoning it. I find that using a combination of salts from Okinawa, Kyushu, and Hyogo gives the resulting soup a more complex flavor. More than likely you won't find the three kinds of Japanese salt I use, so try salts from other countries—anything you particularly like. Taste salts individually and consider how their flavor might work in your soup, and taste them in combination. It will all begin to make sense as you start cooking.

Makes about 650 milliliters (2½ cups)

48 grams (4 tablespoons) sea salt (a combination of 3 or 4 varieties)

340 milliliters (1½ cups) boiling water

275 grams (1 cup) SOFRITO (page 108)

1 Place the salt in a bowl and pour the hot water over it. Stir until it dissolves completely.

2 Mix in the sofrito. Shio tare will keep in the refrigerator for 2 weeks.

SOFRITO

When I first set out to create my bowl of ramen, I tried to do it the way I'd read about and seen other people doing it. I wasn't happy with the results, and my wife told me it was terrible. So I decided that if I wanted to make a bowl of ramen that was personal to me, I had to approach it like any other dish I'd made. Good cooking is good cooking, regardless of whether it's Japanese or American or Puerto Rican. I put aside everything I knew about ramen save for a loose outline, then I fiddled, and read, and ate lots of noodles and lots of French, Spanish, and classical Japanese dishes. Finally, I landed on the idea of using a sofrito as a base. Sofritos are part of many cuisines, especially in Latin America, Spain, and Italy. A sofrito is essentially just small-diced aromatics simmered slowly in oil, and it's used as the basis for various dishes. It became the key component of my shio ramen— the canvas upon which all the other flavors are built.

This recipe makes more than you need for four bowls of ramen. Make the specified amount and reserve the extra for trying new recipes of your own. It's incredibly versatile as a foundation for a dish, or even as a topping.

Makes about 690 grams (2½ cups)

325 grams (11½ ounces) Fuji apples, peeled

1.2 kilos (2½ pounds) yellow onions

160 grams (5½ ounces) garlic

65 grams (2⅓ ounces) fresh ginger, peeled

About 1 liter (1 quart) vegetable oil

1. Preheat the oven to 225°F (110°C).

2. Cut the apples and onions into a small dice. (Or, since everything is going to cook down for hours anyway, you could use a food processor: cut the onions and apples into coarse chunks, then process them separately, pulsing in short bursts to achieve a small dice without turning things into mush.) Dice the garlic and ginger very fine, close to a mince.

3. Put the onions and apples into a deep sauté pan or roasting pan that will hold all the ingredients in a 13-millimeter (½-inch) layer. Pour in the oil, set the pan over medium heat, and cook until the oil begins to bubble and the vegetables begin to sweat. Cover the pan, transfer it to the oven, and cook for about 3 hours. You want the onions and apples to cook very slowly, taking on color only toward the end of cooking. The cooking time will vary depending on how much water is in the onions and apples. Stir the ingredients and rotate the pan regularly to prevent burning.

4 After the onions and apples have cooked down and begun to brown slightly, add the garlic and ginger and continue to cook for another 2 or 3 hours, stirring and rotating the pan from time to time, until everything has a uniformly light brown color and a soft, creamy consistency. Try to prevent the onions and apples from developing dark or crisp edges.

5 Cool the sofrito completely, then refrigerate. It should keep for at least 2 weeks in a tightly sealed container.

Katsuobushi Salt

SHIO RAMEN COMPONENT 3

Katsuobushi is the most commonly used fushi (steamed, smoked, dried, and shaved fish) in Japanese cooking. Along with konbu, it is the foundation of dashi, and by extension, myriad dishes. I love to add the same ingredient at different times and in different guises within a recipe. I find that it deepens the effect of the ingredient without making it too strong. So in addition to the katsuobushi in the dashi, I add katsuobushi powder to each bowl of ramen to really emphasize the smoky fish flavor. I blend the powder with sea salt (and sometimes Parmesan cheese at Ivan Ramen Plus) to create an umami-rich seasoned salt. The likelihood of finding katsuobushi powder in the States is pretty slim, but making it at home is easy. One last note: make sure you give the mixture a good shake before adding it to your ramen, as the salt tends to settle at the bottom of the container.

Makes 20 grams (about ¼ cup)

10 grams (⅓ ounce) katsuobushi (shaved dried bonito)

10 grams (⅓ ounce) sea salt

1 Preheat the oven or a toaster oven to 400°F (200°C).

2 Spread the katsuobushi on a small sheet tray and toast for 3 minutes. Cool, then grind to a powder in a spice grinder or with a mortar and pestle (preferably a Japanese mortar, or suribachi, which is a textured ceramic bowl). You now have katsuobushi powder.

3 Combine the katsuobushi powder with the salt. The mixture will keep in an airtight container in the refrigerator for 3 months.

Double Soup

SHIO RAMEN COMPONENT 4

The only thing I knew for certain when I first began developing my ramen recipe was that it would be a double-soup ramen. I'd fallen in love with the bowl they served at a shop by my kids' school—it was the first place I encountered the double soup upon my return to Tokyo with Mari and the kids. It was lighter than other broths I'd tried, but carried so much complexity and depth of flavor. The double soup literally takes the best of two worlds and combines them.

Chicken stock provides a meaty body to the double soup. I prefer my chicken stock simple and clean, with nothing to distract from the flavor of beautiful Japanese chickens. Dashi brings the umami. I became completely preoccupied with the flavors of dashi during my second stint in Tokyo. The classic dashi used in most Japanese restaurants is made of konbu seaweed and katsuobushi (finely shaved dried bonito). The dashi we make at Ivan Ramen has a great many more ingredients, all in service of an even deeper, umami-rich flavor.

Makes 1 liter (1 quart)

500 milliliters (2 cups)
CHICKEN STOCK (page 114)

500 milliliters (2 cups) DASHI
(page 116)

1 When you're ready to serve the soup, combine the chicken stock and dashi in a saucepan and bring to a simmer over medium-high heat, then turn down the heat to low.

2 Hold at a very gentle simmer, covered, until you're ready to serve, but not for too long—you don't want the liquid to reduce.

CHICKEN STOCK

Ivan Ramen chicken stock is made of whole chickens and water—that's it.

Easy enough, but that also means you should skip those stinky, factory-farmed birds and look for free-range or pasture-raised ones. You'll pay more, but if the only flavor component in this soup is chicken, it's worth paying for chickens that taste good. Buy a whole chicken if you can manage it—meaning with head and feet attached. There's lots of flavor in the ugly bits, along with collagen that gives body to the stock. If you can't find a whole chicken, buy a couple of chicken feet, wash them thoroughly, and throw them in the pot along with the neck and any other parts that come with your bird.

Aside from the quality of the chicken, there are two crucial factors in the success of this soup. The first is maintaining the ratio of water to chicken: there should be twice as much water as chicken by volume, and the liquid level should be maintained over the entire cooking time. The second is temperature. Invest in a thermometer and be vigilant—try to keep the liquid around 176°F (80°C) for the first hour of cooking. This might seem fussy to Americans, and you can just keep it at a gentle simmer if you don't want to monitor the temperature, but very specific temperatures are a hallmark of Japanese soups and stocks. I've made enough soup to tell you confidently that 176°F (80°C) is the right temperature for this stock.

Makes about 5 liters (5 quarts)

1 large (2-kilo/4½-pound) whole chicken (or 2 small whole chickens)

Water

1. Stick your hands into the cavity of the bird and scoop out the giblets and liver, if present. (If you buy from a butcher, you can ask them to do this.) Rinse the bird thoroughly under cold running water. Keep rinsing until the water runs clear. Then trim as much fat as possible from the chicken and reserve.

2. Put the chicken in a large stockpot, along with any giblets, livers, or hearts that came with it. Add enough water (about 5 liters/5 quarts for a 2-kilo/4½-pound bird) to achieve a ratio of about 1 part chicken to 2 parts water by volume. The chicken should be fully submerged in water. Note how far the water level is from the top of the pot. This pot sits on the fire for 6 hours, and you'll want to keep the water at the same level the whole time to yield a light, clean stock.

❸ Over medium heat, heat the water to 176°F (80°C); the water won't be simmering or bubbling, but too hot for you to hold your finger in for more than a second. Keep the water as close to that temperature as possible for 1 hour. Add water as needed to maintain the water level.

❹ After an hour, raise the heat to high and bring the liquid to a slow boil. With a slotted spoon or skimmer, skim all the scum that comes to the surface. When the liquid is clear, pull the bird to the surface with a pair of tongs and very carefully give it a good whack with a wooden spoon. Skim every bit of resulting scum until the stock is completely clear of detritus.

❺ Once you've finished skimming, add the reserved chicken fat to the pot. Lower the heat back to a medium simmer and keep that simmer for the next 5 hours, stirring the pot every 20 minutes and adding water as necessary to maintain the water level. After about 2½ hours, the bird should begin to break down a bit. Press on it with a wooden spoon to help it fall apart. This will extract more flavor into the broth. After 5 hours, the bones and flesh will have mostly fallen apart. Turn off the heat.

❻ Strain the stock through a fine-mesh strainer and discard the meat and bones. Cool the stock, then refrigerate. Once cool, skim the congealed chicken fat from the surface and reserve it for when you need schmaltz for your ramen. Store the stock in an airtight container until you're ready to use it; it will keep for about 1 week in the refrigerator and 1 month in the freezer.

DASHI

There are two stages in this dashi cooking process. The first begins when we soak and simmer konbu (giant seaweed from Hokkaido), iriko niboshi (boiled and sun-dried sardines), and geso (dried squid tentacles) for sweetness. The second stage incorporates four varieties of fushi—fish that have been steamed, deboned, smoked, dried, and shaved extremely thin: mejika (mejika soudabushi), sardine (urume iwashibushi), mackerel (saba-bushi), and bonito (katsuobushi).

Sourcing ingredients and making this dashi can be a serious challenge, and your level of perseverance will determine how well this turns out. I use a special purveyor who gathers the highest quality ingredients from all over Japan. Although the availability of dashi ingredients overseas continues to improve, the likelihood you'll find exactly what I use is slim to none. But this is a no-apologies recipe, meant to give you an exact replica of what I make in Tokyo, as well as to show you my thought process and provoke you to seek out the best available ingredients. Of course, I've also experienced firsthand how hard it is to find this stuff in the States. Often you'll find packages of premixed sardine, mackerel, and bonito flakes—that's fine. A lot of this stuff is available online (see page 205), and in the worst-case scenario, I'm positive you'll at least be able to find katsuobushi; you can use that in place of the other shaved dried fish.

The other nitpicky thing about this recipe is the temperature at which I instruct you to cook the dashi. The Japanese have been making dashi for a long time, obsessing over the specific temperatures that are ideal for extracting all the flavor from the dried fish without disintegrating it into the soup. I've tasted the difference and I agree that it matters. Too hot and the dish can become bitter. You could eyeball it, but I find that there's a wide range of temperatures that people consider to be "simmering," "barely simmering," or even "boiling." It's actually easiest to just use a thermometer.

This recipe will yield around two liters—again, much more than you need for a bowl of ramen. But dashi is an incredibly versatile ingredient and can be used as a direct substitute for meat or chicken stock, as a poaching liquid, or as a base for a vinaigrette. It doesn't freeze well, but once you have dashi in your arsenal, you'll be amazed by how often you find yourself reaching for it.

Makes about 2 liters (2 quarts)

50 grams (2 ounces) konbu

75 grams (2½ ounces) iriko niboshi (dried sardines)

100 grams (3½ ounces) geso (dried squid tentacles)

2.5 liters (10½ cups) water

17 grams (½ ounce) urume iwashibushi (shaved dried sardines)

17 grams (½ ounce) sababushi (shaved dried mackerel)

17 grams (½ ounce) mejika soudabushi (shaved dried mejika)

17 grams (½ ounce) katsuobushi (shaved dried bonito)

1. Wipe the seaweed with a damp cloth and place it in a large bowl with the dried sardines and the dried squid tentacles. Cover with cool water and let soak for at least 2 hours, or overnight, in the refrigerator.

2. Drain the soaked seaweed, sardines, and squid tentacles, place them in a large stockpot, and cover with the water. Over medium heat, bring the water up to 140°F (60°C). Once it reaches temperature, skim all of the scum from the surface, then strain the liquid through a fine-mesh strainer. Gently press the strained ingredients against the sides of the strainer to extract as much liquid as possible. Discard the solids.

3. Pour the liquid into a clean pot. Over medium heat, heat it to 176°F (80°C), and hold it as close to that temperature as possible. Add the shaved sardines, mackerel, and mejika and cook for 5 minutes, then add the shaved bonito and cook for another 3 minutes, keeping the liquid at 176°F (80°C) the whole time.

4. Strain the liquid again through a fine-mesh sieve, again gently pushing down on the ingredients to extract as much liquid as possible. Discard the solids.

5. Cool the liquid to room temperature, then store in the refrigerator. Dashi doesn't have the best shelf life—it keeps for a couple days in the refrigerator—so make this as close to the day you'll use it as possible.

Toasted Rye Noodles

SHIO RAMEN COMPONENT 5

Our noodle recipe has changed over the years. The noodle we serve now isn't the same as the one we opened with. This recipe is my play on soba; these can be served hot or cold. Most ramen shops would frown upon using soba-style noodles because they're so mild compared to a salty, porky ramen broth. But my soup is lighter than most, and works well with these more ethereal noodles.

I'm personally obsessed with the kaori, or aroma, of the noodles. Most shops use one type of flour that is specifically designed for ramen, with a protein level of 10 to 11 percent. These flours are inexpensive, but they don't have the deep, fresh aroma that I'm looking for. At my shop, we combine soft udon flour (7 to 8 percent protein), with high-protein bread flour (14 to 15 percent protein) and a small percentage of rye or other whole grain flour, for a noodle with an irresistible aroma of fresh wheat. It's a circuitous route to get to the 10 to 11 percent protein content that works for noodles, but we get much more interesting textures and complex flavors, and even a deeper color, with pretty little speckles of whole grain. Toasting the flour brings out more aromatic nuances, while removing some of the liquid in the flour and making for an even chewier noodle.

Powdered kansui adds the alkaline component of these noodles. As noted in numerous places by Harold McGee, the oracle of culinary science, a simple substitute for kansui powder is baked baking soda. Spread baking soda in a thin layer on a foil-lined sheet tray and bake for one hour at 275°F (135°C). Store in a container with a tight-fitting lid for up to a couple of months.

(CONTINUED)

(CONTINUED)

In Tokyo, we work with an excellent and very expensive noodle machine. You won't have one. But neither did I when I first started developing these recipes. Believe me, you can make great ramen noodles at home with a manual pasta machine. But it will take you more than one try to iron out the kinks. Try the recipe, curse me out if you must, and try again. Your kitchen will produce different results than mine—that's just the reality of cooking, Repeat and tinker with the proportions until you have your ideal bowl of toothsome, fragrant noodles. This recipe yields enough noodles for ten bowls of ramen.

Makes about 1.3 kilos (2¾ pounds)

75 grams (½ cup) rye flour

620 grams (4 cups) high-gluten (14 to 15 percent protein) bread flour

300 grams (2 cups) cake flour

10 grams (1½ teaspoons) kansui powder (see note, page 119)

430 milliliters (1¾ cups) cool water

13 grams (1 tablespoon) salt

Cornstarch

1. Toast the rye flour in a nonstick pan over medium-high heat. Stir the flour until a few wisps of fragrance reach your nose, about 4 minutes. Don't give it any color! Weigh the flour again after it's been toasted: you only want 70 grams of toasted flour for this recipe—the extra 5 grams are to account for any loss while toasting.

2. In the bowl of a stand mixer, combine the flours and set aside. Ramen noodle dough can be quite stiff and difficult to work with. If you don't have a stand mixer, good old-fashioned elbow grease will have to do.

3. In a separate bowl, slowly stir the kansui into the water until it's fully dissolved (this takes a little time). Then stir in the salt to dissolve.

4. Outfit your mixer with the dough hook attachment. With the mixer running on low speed, add the water in thirds to the flour mixture. After a few minutes, the dough should begin to come together. It will be a bit shaggy—more so than Italian pasta dough. If it isn't coming together at all, add a spoonful of water. Once it comes together, increase the speed to medium-low and let the machine run for 10 minutes, until the dough forms a ball. Turn off the mixer and cover the dough with plastic wrap. Let stand for 30 minutes.

5 After 30 minutes, the dough should be significantly softer in texture and smoother in appearance. Set the dough ball on a cutting board, flatten it with the palm of your hand, then cut it into four 5-centimeter (2-inch) strips. Cover the dough strips with a damp kitchen towel.

6 Set up your pasta machine and adjust it for the largest size. Pass one piece of dough through the machine, then fold it over on itself so that you have a double sheet. Turn the machine to the second largest size, and run the doubled sheet through. Double the sheet over again, and run it through the third largest setting.

7 Don't double the sheet over again. Run it through the fourth largest setting, then once through the smallest setting. Set aside and repeat with the remaining pieces of dough. Once the sheets are all rolled, pass them through the thinnest cutter you have, or cut them by hand so that they are as thin as possible. As you work, toss the noodles with a little cornstarch to keep them from sticking together, and shake off the excess before cooking. Store the noodles in a container wrapped tightly with plastic (or individual portions in ziplock bags) for up to a day.

Menma

SHIO RAMEN COMPONENT 6

Menma is cured bamboo shoot, usually cut from the bottom part of the shoot. Menma is a love-it-or-hate-it thing, and to be honest, they aren't my personal favorite. As a result, they're the only thing coming out of my kitchen that I don't make from scratch. At Ivan Ramen, we serve hosaki menma, which are taken from the very tip of the shoot. They have a milder, fresher taste, and are more tender than menma from the bottom of the shoot. Plus, they're long and thin—perfect for being slurped up with noodles. Since we started serving hosaki menma, it's become quite common in Tokyo.

You can find prepared menma in a jar in most Japanese grocery stores, but in case you can't, I've provided the following recipe that uses the chewier kind of bamboo shoot that's more common in America. It won't be quite as crunchy as the stuff at Ivan Ramen in Tokyo, but it's still delicious. You can buy sliced, uncured bamboo shoots in two styles: 1) packed in water, in which case they just need to be rinsed; or 2) packed in salt, in which case they must be soaked in water for a day. You're almost always going to end up with more menma than you need for your ramen. I've included some alternative uses for the extra on pages 155 and 156.

Makes about 500 grams (1 pound)

500 grams (1 pound) sliced, uncured bamboo shoots

750 milliliters (3 cups) water

❶ Rinse the bamboo shoots if they're packed in water. If they're packed in salt, soak them in water for a day, changing the water a few times during the course of the soak.

❷ Combine the water, katsuobushi, and konbu in a bowl and soak for 1 hour. **(CONTINUED)**

30 grams (1 ounce)
katsuobushi (shaved
dried bonito)

5 grams (¼ ounce) konbu

100 milliliters (½ cup) sake

50 milliliters (3½ tablespoons)
soy sauce

40 milliliters (2½ tablespoons)
mirin

20 grams (1½ tablespoons)
sugar

(CONTINUED)

3 Strain the water from the katsuobushi and konbu into a saucepan, and discard the katsuobushi and konbu. Add the sake, soy sauce, and mirin. Bring to a boil over high heat, then reduce to the heat to maintain a simmer and cook, uncovered, for 10 minutes. Stir in the sugar until it's dissolved. Add the bamboo shoots and simmer for 10 minutes longer.

4 Let the menma come to room temperature, then refrigerate in its cooking liquid until ready to use. Menma will keep for a week in the refrigerator.

Pork Belly Chashu

SHIO RAMEN COMPONENT 7

At Ivan Ramen, we're renowned for the big, thick slices of succulent chashu that rest on top of our noodles. Chashu is Chinese-style, soy-and-sugar-seasoned pork. The definition is a loose one, and can refer to either pork belly or pork shoulder. (Some of the more decadent shops serve both in the same bowl.) The meat is usually brined in a soy-based marinade (chashu tare) or braised in a richly flavored soy-based broth. Some shops poach the pork in their soup broth before adding it to the marinade in order to doubly reap the benefits of the meat's flavor. Sometimes you'll find chashu sliced extremely thick; other times it's sliced thinly and piled on. A few places char the meat with a blowtorch before it goes into the bowl.

Our shio ramen soup is a strictly chicken-and-fish-based one, so when I first set out to make my chashu, I knew I needed a meaty counterpoint that would scream, "Pork!" I went through six types of pork belly with our butcher, Fukuya-san, before finally settling on the breed I liked. Good pork belly needs to have multiple even layers of meat and fat. Do your best to find a high-quality cut.

Finally, there's something universally attractive about a fat hunk of pork belly melting into a hot bowl of soup, but this is equally true outside the bowl—chashu is fantastic over a bowl of rice, in a sandwich, or pan-fried until crispy. Keep in mind that I purposely keep the soy, sugar, ginger, and garlic on the lighter side so as not to interfere with the flavor of the soup and noodles. If you want more flavorful pork belly for nonsoup applications, feel free to replace some of the water in the braise with more chashu tare.

(CONTINUED)

Makes about 1 kilo (2 pounds)—a big slab

25 milliliters (1½ tablespoons) sake

25 milliliters (1½ tablespoons) mirin

10 grams (2 teaspoons) garlic, chopped coarsely

15 grams (1 tablespoon) fresh ginger, peeled and chopped coarsely

135 milliliters (½ cup + 1 tablespoon) dark soy sauce

75 milliliters (⅓ cup) light soy sauce

15 grams (1 tablespoon) sugar

1 (1-kilo/2-pound) piece of pork belly

Water

(CONTINUED)

1 Measure the sake and mirin into a saucepan and heat it to a light simmer over medium heat. Cook for 3 minutes to burn off some of the alcohol.

2 Add the garlic, ginger, and two soy sauces to the pan and bring the mixture back to a simmer over medium heat. Add the sugar and stir until it dissolves, about 30 seconds. Continue cooking, uncovered, over medium heat for 5 minutes, then turn off the heat, and let the mixture sit for at least an hour, to allow the flavors to meld.

3 Remove the meat from the refrigerator 1 hour before cooking to allow it to come closer to room temperature. Completely cold meat cooks more slowly, and you'll risk drying out the exterior before the interior cooks.

4 Cut the pork belly in half across the grain and put it in a pot that will hold it snugly. Pour in the cooled chashu tare and then add enough water to just cover the pork by about 1 centimeter (½ inch).

5 Over high heat, bring the liquid up to a full boil. Skim off any scum that comes to the surface. Lower the heat to a gentle simmer and cook, covered, until the meat is tender enough that it is easily pulled apart with a fork, between 2½ and 4 hours. In my experience, mass-produced pork belly takes longer to cook than small farm–produced pork belly, so the cooking time will depend on your cut of meat.

6 When the meat is tender, remove it from the pot and set it on a tray to cool. Reserve the cooking liquid for future braises or for the eggs on page 131; it will keep for a week in the fridge or you can freeze it for 2 months.

7 Once the meat has cooled down to room temperature, refrigerate it until it's completely chilled, or up to 5 days. It's important to chill the belly thoroughly before slicing

it, or you'll end up with pulled pork. Once it's cooled, slice the belly into strips across the grain, then into pieces of the desired thickness. I like 1-centimeter (1/2-inch) slices. You can reheat the pork and use it however you see fit. I reheat my pork belly in simmering water or stock for a minute to keep the flavor clean.

Half-Cooked Eggs

SHIO RAMEN COMPONENT 8

I **really obsessed over the eggs.** For a long time, eggs weren't a traditional ramen topping; they were offered hardboiled and unpeeled in a basket for customers to pluck out and eat while they waited, or to add to their soup. As ramen became more refined and less junk-foody, cooks started to treat the eggs with a more care. The eggs they sell in Japan are beyond delicious, and to me, they're an indispensable part of a bowl of ramen. We serve hanjuku tamago, half-cooked eggs that have a firm but soft white and a mostly liquid yolk.

My search for perfect eggs took me to innumerable egg farms. After an extensive search, I found one that tasted great, had the most brilliant orange yolks, and peeled easily. (Believe me, when you have to peel two hundred eggs a day, that's an important criterion.) Then I spent almost as much time figuring out how to cook the eggs properly as I did perfecting the noodles. But I've got it now: punch a pinhole in the bottom, boil for 6 minutes and 10 seconds, stirring gently for the first 2 minutes, then ice immediately. Once they're cool, the eggs are peeled and soaked in a light shoyu tare (or, preferably, reserved chashu cooking liquid; see page 127). Sliced in half and served at room temperature atop the ramen, the eggs are a perfect supporting cast member for the soup and noodles, adding an extra touch of color and unctuousness to the bowl.

Makes 6 eggs

50 milliliters (3½ tablespoons) sake

50 milliliters (3½ tablespoons) mirin

① Simmer the sake and mirin in a saucepan over medium-high heat for 2 minutes to cook off a bit of the alcohol. Reduce the heat to low, then add the soy sauce, sugar, garlic, and ginger and simmer and stir for 10 minutes. Let come to room temperature; you can store the mixture in the refrigerator for up to a week. **(CONTINUED)**

200 milliliters (1¾ cup + 1 tablespoon) soy sauce

30 grams (2 tablespoons) sugar

40 grams (3 tablespoons) garlic, chopped coarsely

75 grams (2½ ounces) fresh ginger, chopped coarsely

6 room-temperature fresh large eggs

1 liter (1 quart) water

(CONTINUED)

2 Bring a large pot of water to a boil. You want a big pot so that when the eggs go in, the temperature won't drop too drastically, and the water will quickly come back to a boil.

3 Poke a small hole in the bottom (larger end) of each egg with a pushpin.

4 Gently slide the eggs into the boiling water. Start your timer. Stir for the first 2 minutes. Prepare a large bowl of ice water to shock the eggs.

5 The total cooking time for a large egg in Tokyo is 6 minutes and 10 seconds. You might decide to adjust that time depending on the size of your eggs, how many you're cooking, or what the chickens were thinking about when they laid them.

6 Remove the eggs after 6 minutes and 10 seconds, and immediately place them in the ice bath. Stir until there are no pockets of hot water.

7 In a large bowl, combine the shoyu tare with the liter of water. When the eggs are cooled completely—after about 15 minutes—peel and soak them in the seasoning liquid for 2 hours in the refrigerator. The eggs will hold in the soak for 3 days.

8 When it comes time to slice the eggs and add them to the ramen, a taut nylon fishing line gets the job done without losing any of the precious yolk.

Now What?

You've successfully made a complete bowl of ramen, or maybe just a big batch of dashi. Now you've got a bunch of leftovers on your hands. All that time spent sweating vegetables and simmering stock, and now you don't know what to do with all this stuff. The thought of throwing it away is heartbreaking.

Have no fear. Most of the meals I've eaten for the past five years have included some component lifted from my ramen recipe. This section illustrates how to repurpose dashi, chicken stock, sofrito, chashu (although you should probably be able to figure that one out yourself), fat, and menma. Nothing will go to waste, especially if you decide to get a little creative yourself. I encourage you to start swapping dashi in recipes that call for stock, cooking in chicken and pork fat, sneaking sofrito into other soups and braises, and painting grilled meats with shio tare.

Nothing's sacred! I won't be offended if you find that you like chashu in tacos better than you like it in soup. Becoming a better cook is all about finding the best way to use what you've got on hand.

Flavored Fat

ANOTHER USE FOR FAT

We use copious amounts of chicken and pork fat at Ivan Ramen. By flavoring the fats with herbs or other aromatics, you can change the entire flavor profile of a dish. At Ivan Ramen, we flavor pork fat with negi (Japanese green onions) and ginger; at Ivan Ramen Plus, we use lemon-infused chicken fat as a fragrant garnish. If you've got extra fat on hand, you can experiment by taking a cup and gently cooking it in a small saucepan for an hour with a few sprigs of your preferred herb and/or a few garlic cloves.

Use these fats to sauté vegetables or finish grilled meats or stews with a drizzle of flavored fat and a sprinkle of sea salt. If you've got loads of uncooked fat on hand, multiply the following recipes, and you'll have an aromatic bath for confit (meat cooked slowly in its own fat).

Sometimes I feel guilty about how often I utilize these fats—it feels a bit like cheating—like I'm trying to make up for missing flavor with delicious fat. But fat tastes better than other cheats, like MSG, and used appropriately it really elevates food to a new level of deliciousness.

GARLIC AND ANCHOVY PORK FAT

Makes about 235 milliliters (1 cup)

235 milliliters (1 cup)
PORK FAT (page 105)

3 cloves garlic

3 cured anchovies

❶ Combine the ingredients in a small saucepan and simmer over the lowest heat possible for an hour.

❷ Cool to room temperature and store (with the garlic and anchovies) in an airtight container in the refrigerator for up to a week.

HERBED CHICKEN FAT

*Makes about
235 milliliters (1 cup)*

235 milliliters (1 cup)
CHICKEN FAT (page 104)

2 sprigs thyme

2 sprigs rosemary

❶ Combine the ingredients in a small saucepan and simmer over the lowest heat possible for an hour.

❷ Cool to room temperature, strain, and store in an airtight container in the refrigerator for up to a week.

Schmaltz-Fried Chicken Katsu

ANOTHER USE FOR CHICKEN FAT

I**t's such a simple idea, but when was the last time** you fried chicken in its own fat? You could be buying organic chickens and making your own breadcrumbs, but if you just fry chicken in vegetable oil, you're missing a big flavor opportunity.

All over Tokyo, you'll find tonkatsu shops serving fried, breaded pork cutlets. This is a slight variation using chicken, but I still serve it with traditional accompaniments of tonkatsu sauce (I like Bulldog brand), a heaping pile of finely shredded cabbage, and a mound of Japanese short-grain rice. Add a bowl of miso soup, and you've got a classic Tokyo diner dish that I ate countless times during my first stint in Japan. Cook this for your family, and somewhere, a young, aimless Ivan Orkin with poor Japanese skills will be smiling upon you.

Makes 4 servings

4 (150-gram/5-ounce) skinless, boneless chicken breasts

500 milliliters (2 cups) cold water

28 grams (2 tablespooons + 1 teaspoon) salt, plus additional for seasoning

1 clove garlic, crushed

½ head green cabbage

170 grams (½ cup) all-purpose flour

2 large eggs

1 Place each breast between two sheets of plastic wrap or parchment paper. Pound the breast flat using a meat mallet or the bottom of a saucepan until it's uniformly about 13 millimeters (½ inch) thick.

2 Mix together the water, salt, and garlic, and stir until the salt dissolves. (This quick brine is a great flavoring agent that you can use with any meat when your time is short.) Add the chicken to the brine and soak for 30 minutes while you prepare the other ingredients.

3 Shred the cabbage with a sharp knife or mandoline; reserve in a bowl of cold water.

4 Place the flour, eggs, and panko in three separate shallow vessels. Beat the eggs. **(CONTINUED)**

80 grams (1½ cups) panko

240 milliliters (1 cup)
CHICKEN FAT (page 104)

700 milliliters (3 cups)
vegetable oil

Warm STEAMED RICE
(page 191), for serving

Bottled tonkatsu sauce,
for serving

(CONTINUED)

5 Remove the breasts from the brine and quickly pat them
dry. Dredge each breast in the flour and shake off the
excess. Next, give the breasts a quick dip in the egg, again
shaking off any excess. Finally, coat the breasts with
panko. Press the breadcrumbs onto the meat to form a
solid crust.

6 Choose a sauté pan large enough to hold one or two of the
chicken breasts, and tall enough that the fat can cover
the meat completely with plenty of room to spare. Heat the
chicken fat and vegetable oil in the pan over medium
heat to 350°F (176°C), then carefully slide in 1 or 2 breasts,
depending on how many fit in your pan. Fry until crisp
and browned on both sides, 3 to 4 minutes per side.
Remove the fried breasts to a paper towel–lined plate
and season with salt. Cook the remaining breasts in
the same way.

7 Drain the cabbage well.

8 Serve the chicken with rice and a pile of cabbage on the
side. Drizzle tonkatsu sauce all over everything.

Chicken Teriyaki

ANOTHER USE FOR CHICKEN FAT

Although in America anything "teriyaki" sounds a little mundane or contrived, this really is a staple in Japanese homes. I make it often for the kids, because a) I always have tons of chicken fat on hand, and b) it's delicious, so why not?

Makes 4 servings

1 kilo (2 pounds) skinless, boneless chicken thighs

15 grams (1 tablespoon) all-purpose flour

Salt

30 milliliters (2 tablespoons) CHICKEN FAT (page 104)

120 milliliters (½ cup) sake

120 milliliters (½ cup) mirin

20 milliliters (4 teaspoons) soy sauce

15 grams (1 tablespoon) sugar

Warm STEAMED RICE (page 191), for serving

Shredded green cabbage, for serving

1 Toss the thighs with the flour and 1 teaspoon of salt.

2 In a medium sauté pan over high heat, brown the chicken in the chicken fat (it won't be cooked through), working in batches to avoid crowding the pan and to keep the meat from steaming rather than sautéing. Set aside, then pour off half of the fat but leave any browned bits in the pan.

3 In a bowl, mix together the sake, mirin, and soy sauce, then add the sugar and mix until completely dissolved.

4 Return the chicken to the pan over medium-high heat and pour the sauce on top. Scrape loose any bits from the bottom of the pan. Cook over medium heat until the thighs are cooked through and the sauce is reduced to a syrupy consistency, about 12 minutes. Serve over rice and shredded cabbage.

Omu Raisu

ANOTHER USE FOR SOFRITO

Omu raisu (rice omelet) is one of the most popular dishes in Japan, both at home and in restaurants. To Western ears it doesn't sound immediately compelling—lightly fried rice laced with ketchup and covered with a sheet of runny eggs. It's slathered with more ketchup to finish, which is probably why I jumped on the bandwagon almost immediately and have never looked back. My childhood recollections don't include any warm and fuzzy comfort dishes, so when I feel down and out or just need some food love, this is the dish I invariably turn to.

Using sofrito as the base for the rice filling gives it a luxurious silky texture and depth of flavor that it doesn't always have. You can incorporate any veggie or meat that you like. I've used the classics. As far as I'm concerned, this dish is a vehicle for runny eggs and loads of ketchup.

Makes 4 servings

140 grams (½ cup) SOFRITO (page 108)

150 grams (5 ounces) skinless, boneless chicken breast, cut into very small dice

720 grams (4 cups) STEAMED RICE (page 191) (day-old rice is fine)

100 grams (3½ ounces) frozen peas

Lots of ketchup

8 large eggs

Vegetable oil spray

1 In a wide sauté pan set over medium-high heat, warm the sofrito until it starts to sizzle, then add the chicken and cook through, about 4 minutes.

2 Add the rice. Mix and stir until the rice, sofrito, and chicken are thoroughly incorporated. Add the peas, cook for a minute, then start squirting in the ketchup. This is the most gratifying moment for ketchup lovers like me. Squirt it in to your taste, but it shouldn't be so wet that you just get a mouthful of ketchup. It should look like red fried rice, with a touch of moisture from the ketchup. Remove from the heat and season with salt and pepper to taste.

3 Fill a small bowl with rice and pack it down. Upend the bowl onto a plate to create a molehill of rice in the center of the plate. Repeat for each serving. **(CONTINUED)**

(CONTINUED)

4 In a small bowl, whip 2 eggs until frothy.

5 Heat a medium nonstick skillet over medium-high heat until a drop of egg sizzles in the pan. Spray the pan with vegetable spray and pour in the beaten eggs. Rock the pan gently so that the eggs coat the bottom of the pan. The eggs should cook quite quickly. Lift a corner with a spatula to allow the uncooked egg that has pooled on top to run into the exposed area. You're aiming for a sheet of fluffy cooked egg with a little bit of undercooked egg remaining on top.

6 Slide the omelet over the mound of rice. If you've done this perfectly, you now have a "handkerchief" of egg on top of the rice. To gild the lily, tuck the edges of the omelet under the rice to create a neat package. Squeeze ketchup all over the omelet and plate.

7 Repeat the whole process for the other plates. If you're living in a Japanese household like mine, everyone starts eating as soon as their dish lands in front of them. This would have driven my father insane, which makes it all the better.

Ozoni

ANOTHER USE FOR DOUBLE SOUP

As much as I wished they were, my holidays as a child in the Orkin household were not the wondrous food spectacles of my famished imagination. So when I married into a Japanese family, I eagerly adopted the various Japanese holidays and the celebratory foods that come along with them. Japanese New Year is my favorite. We spend several days preparing for it, so that on New Year's Day we can start drinking in the morning and eat without doing any work. (It's like Saturday Sabbath for Jews, but rather than worshipping God, we spend the day tying one on.)

Of all the Oshogatsu (New Year's) specialty dishes, ozoni is the best. It's super simple: chicken soup lightly flavored with dashi, pieces of chicken, carrot, mitsuba (an aromatic herb), and crisp baked or grilled mochi (glutinous rice cakes). The stretchy, chewy hot cakes soften in the broth and impart a little smokiness. You can buy mochi at any Japanese grocer.

Every family in Japan makes this dish a little differently, but no matter what, it's the ideal way to start the New Year. Try this recipe once as is, then have fun swapping in whatever vegetables you like. This dish is usually served along with several others. You can easily make this into an entrée by doubling the recipe.

Makes 4 servings

4 fresh shiitake mushrooms, cleaned and trimmed

1 (5-centimeter/2-inch) piece of daikon, peeled

1 medium carrot, peeled

500 milliliters (2 cups) CHICKEN STOCK (page 114)

500 milliliters (2 cups) DASHI (page 116) or AGO DASHI (page 179)

❶ Preheat a toaster oven (or full-size oven, if you must) to 400°F (200°C).

❷ Cut a shallow X into the top of each mushroom. Thinly slice the daikon into rounds, then cut each round into 4 wedges. Thinly slice the carrot on the bias.

❸ Combine the chicken stock, dashi, soy sauce, sake, and mirin in a saucepan and bring to a simmer. Add the chicken, mushrooms, daikon, and carrots, and simmer gently until everything is cooked through—about 10 minutes. **(CONTINUED)**

5 milliliters (1 teaspoon)
soy sauce

15 milliliters (1 tablespoon)
sake

15 milliliters (1 tablespoon)
mirin

100 grams (3½ ounces) skinless,
boneless chicken thigh, sliced
into bite-size chunks and
seasoned with salt

4 squares of mochi, plus
additional for snacking

4 sprigs mitsuba (Japanese
wild parsley) or celery leaves

(CONTINUED)

4 Bake the mochi directly on the oven rack until they become puffy, and the edges turn golden brown, about 10 minutes.

5 Set out four small bowls and divide the soup among them. Put a mochi cake into each bowl, garnish with mitsuba, and serve.

Dashi Maki Tamago

ANOTHER USE FOR DASHI

This fluffy, layered, slightly sweet omelet is served in market stalls throughout Japan, and has an important place on the table at New Year's Day celebratory feasts. The omelet is a mixture of eggs, dashi, and soy sauce, cooked in a rectangular pan in thin layers that are rolled up over one another. You can find a rectangular pan in a Japanese market, but don't kill yourself over it—you can still make a fine omelet in a round skillet.

Makes 1 omelet

3 large eggs

5 milliliters (1 teaspoon) soy sauce, plus additional for serving

20 grams (1½ tablespoons) sugar

90 milliliters (6 tablespoons) DASHI (page 116)

Vegetable oil spray

80 grams (½ cup) grated peeled daikon, for serving

1 In a bowl, thoroughly whisk together the eggs, soy sauce, sugar, and dashi. Set aside.

2 Heat a small nonstick skillet (preferably a rectangular one) over medium-low heat and spray with oil. Pour in just enough egg mixture to coat the bottom of the pan. When the egg is half set, use a rubber spatula or a pair of chopsticks to begin folding it over on itself, starting at the side closest to you with a fold of about 2 centimeters (¾ inch). Continue folding/rolling until you reach the end of the pan.

3 Pour more egg mixture into the empty side of the pan, just enough to cover the bottom. Lift the already-rolled omelet to allow some of the uncooked egg mixture to run underneath. Repeat the rolling procedure, this time beginning with the other end, so you're rolling the second omelet around the first. Keep the heat low enough that the egg is not becoming crisp and brown, but rather staying soft and creamy. **(CONTINUED)**

(CONTINUED)

4 Repeat step 3 until you've used all your egg mixture or the omelet is too big to roll. (This will depend on the size of the pan you've chosen.)

5 Turn the omelet out onto a plate and allow it to cool and set. If you have a bamboo sushi roller, wrap it in plastic wrap, roll the omelet inside, and exert a little pressure to form the omelet into a perfect rectangular shape. In lieu of a bamboo roller, you could use a piece of heavy-duty aluminum foil.

6 Once the omelet has cooled to room temperature, cut it in 2-centimeter (1-inch) slices and serve with grated daikon drizzled with soy sauce.

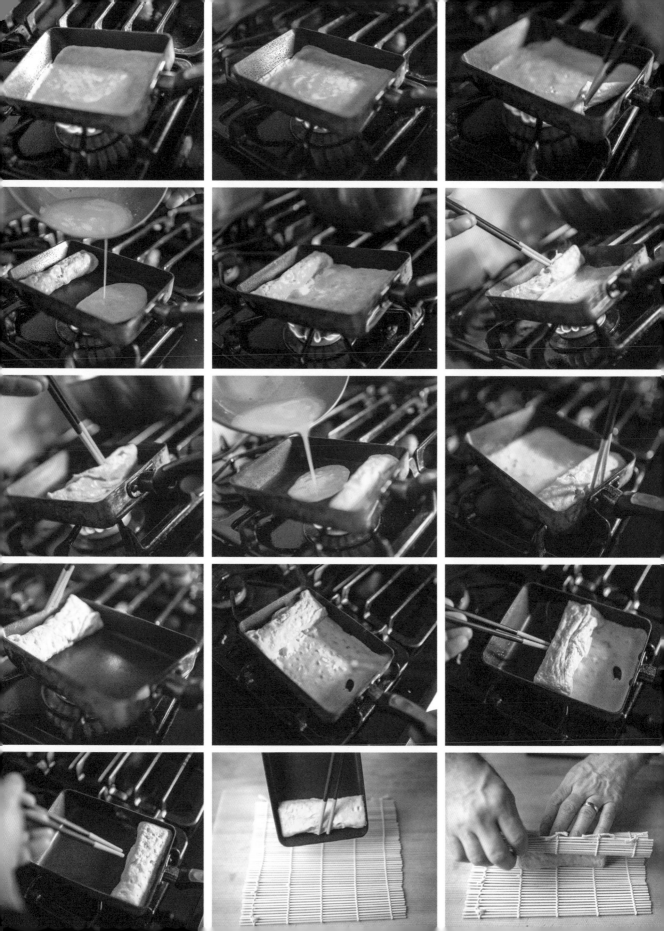

Cold Tofu with Menma

ANOTHER USE FOR MENMA, CHASHU, AND DASHI

The simplest way to utilize a surplus of menma is to eat a pile while drinking beer. If you're not into acting like a panda bear, scarfing a pile of cured bamboo, then this dish and the next are for two simple cooked dishes that make use of extra menma.

Makes 4 servings

1 (400-gram/14-ounce) block silken tofu, drained

200 grams (7 ounces) MENMA (page 123)

100 grams (3½ ounces) warm PORK BELLY CHASHU (page 127), sliced into thin strips

4 green onions, cut thin on the bias

5 milliliters (1 teaspoon) DASHI (page 116)

15 milliliters (1 tablespoon) good-quality toasted sesame oil (I like Kadoya brand)

Sea salt

1. Slice the tofu into 4 pieces and place them in the center of 4 small plates.

2. Combine the remaining ingredients—menma, chashu, green onions, dashi, and sesame oil—in a bowl. Season to taste with salt.

3. Put a small pile of the menma mixture on top of each piece of tofu. Drizzle any remaining liquid over the top of each dish and serve.

Menma Sauté

ANOTHER USE FOR MENMA

Regular chives are not a great alternative here; try green onions if you can't find nira (Japanese chives). And make sure your bean sprouts are fresh and not slimy.

Makes 4 appetizer servings

50 milliliters (3½ tablespoons) sake

50 milliliters (3½ tablespoons) mirin

50 milliliters (3½ tablespoons) soy sauce

15 grams (1 tablespoon) sugar

15 milliliters (1 tablespoon) sesame oil

500 grams (1 pound) bean sprouts, rinsed

200 grams (7 ounces) MENMA (page 123)

1 bunch nira (Japanese or Chinese chives), cut in 2-centimeter (1-inch) pieces

2 cloves garlic, minced

❶ In a small bowl, mix together the sake, mirin, soy sauce, and sugar, stirring until the sugar is fully dissolved. Set aside.

❷ Heat a medium sauté pan over high heat and add the sesame oil. When the oil is hot and shimmering, add the bean sprouts, menma, and nira. Sauté for 2 minutes, then add the garlic. Sauté for 2 minutes more, then add the sake-mirin-soy mixture. Let it bubble up and reduce for 2 minutes, then serve.

Chashu Cubano

ANOTHER USE FOR CHASHU AND PORK FAT

Life is pretty good if your biggest problem is having too much slow-cooked pork belly on hand. The chashu recipe on page 127 yields much more than you need for four bowls of ramen, so you'll have enough to make other things like this over-the-top Cuban sandwich.

The Cubano has become a mainstream thing, but if it's not done well, you're better off with a PB&J. The importance of garlic mayo cannot be overstated; depending on how much mayo you like on your sandwich, you may have extra for future use. It will keep in the fridge for at least a couple weeks. (There are worse fates.) Wrapping the chashu with ham and Swiss cheese takes the pork to the next dimension. There's no need to get fancy with the bread—your favorite cheap hero roll is the perfect vehicle for a Cubano.

Makes 4 sandwiches

20 grams (1 tablespoon) roasted garlic from ROASTED GARLIC AND GARLIC OIL, (page 158)

4 cloves raw garlic, minced

30 milliliters (2 tablespoons) garlic oil from ROASTED GARLIC AND GARLIC OIL (page 158)

175 grams (1 cup) mayonnaise

Salt and pepper

4 (15-centimeter/6-inch) hero rolls

8 (13-millimeter/½-inch) slices PORK BELLY CHASHU (page 127), warmed through in its cooking liquid

❶ Make garlic mayo by mixing the roasted and raw garlic, garlic oil, and mayonnaise together in a bowl. Season with salt and pepper to taste.

❷ Slice open the rolls and slather both sides of the interior with an (un)healthy amount of garlic mayo. Layer on the warm chashu, ham, Swiss cheese, and pickles. Close the sandwiches and brush the tops generously with pork fat.

❸ Heat a panini press or a skillet over medium-high heat until very hot. Place a sandwich in the press or skillet. If you're using a skillet, weigh down the sandwiches with a brick wrapped in foil, or press down firmly on it with a large metal spatula. **(CONTINUED)**

8 slices good-quality
cured ham

8 slices Swiss cheese

2 dill pickles, cut into
thin rounds

PORK FAT (page 105)

(CONTINUED)

❹ Flip the sandwich when the first side is crisp and golden,
about 3 minutes. Repeat on the second side. Toast the rest
of the sandwiches, serving them hot as they come out of
the pan.

ROASTED GARLIC AND GARLIC OIL

This garlic isn't really roasted, just poached in oil until very soft. All I do is put garlic cloves
in a pot, cover them with oil, and cook at a low temperature until they're golden and soft—
about 2 hours. This yields two very versatile products: roasted garlic puree and garlic oil.
I use vegetable oil, which makes everything vegetarian, but this is a golden opportunity to
substitute schmaltz or pork fat. Animal-based garlic fat will drive a person berserk with lust,
perk up any dish, and make you a god among men. But I digress.

If you don't have two hours to spare, throw a handful of garlic cloves into a small pot,
cover with oil, and cook over medium heat just until the garlic starts to color. The garlic
won't be as soft, but you can chop it up, and the oil will still be fragrant.

*Makes 250 grams
(9 ounces) of garlic
and 500 milliliters
(2 cups) oil*

500 milliliters (2 cups)
vegetable oil (or a different
fat of your choosing)

250 grams (9 ounces) peeled
garlic cloves

❶ Combine the oil and garlic in a small pot, and set over the
lowest heat you can. If you have a heat diffuser, all the better. Keep the pot on the heat until the garlic cloves can be
smashed easily—about 2 hours. Carefully monitor the heat;
the oil should bubble lightly, but if it simmers, the garlic
browns quickly and gets tough. Remove the pan from the
heat for a minute if you sense it's getting too hot.

❷ Strain the garlic from the oil and reserve. Puree the cloves
with a hand blender, a mortar and pestle, or a fork. Add a
little oil to facilitate the process. Let both oil and puree cool
to room temperature before storing in the fridge. Now you
have fragrant garlic oil and sweet, aromatic garlic paste.

Variations on a Noodle

When Ivan Ramen first opened, shio ramen was the only thing on the menu. For me, shio ramen encapsulates everything that's great about ramen—the purity of flavor, the attention to detail, the balance of salty and fatty and meaty. My shio ramen defined me as a ramen chef and put the restaurant on the map.

There are dozens of ramen variations—from shoyu (soy sauce) ramen, to miso ramen, to tonkotsu (ultra-rich pork broth), to mazemen (just a little soup), to tsukemen (noodles and separate dipping sauce). Of all the major types of Japanese food, ramen is the only one without a rigid set of regulations dictating its preparation. Soba, udon, sushi, kaiseki—these are all things that are meant to be made a certain way. To step outside the rules is heresy. But ramen didn't grow from a grand, ancient tradition, so it allows for creativity and experimentation.

I worked in a soba shop for a month. The owner was nice and let me make the noodles, but I hated it. I hated the way you have to make soba. I hated the rigid stance I had to assume when I was kneading, and the specific way I had to touch the dough. (Learning classical French food can feel the same way.) I didn't like the rules and the whole Zen aspect of it. But I did really like making noodles and working with dough.

As my shops grew in popularity and reputation, I felt more confident dabbling with other styles. Some of these experiments went awry. (I once made a Mexican taco mazemen, and to this day I maintain that it was fucking brilliant. I toasted guajillo chiles and blended them with pork fat for the soup, and topped it with a bean and spicy pork thing, shredded iceberg, tomatoes, chipotles, and negi. Everybody hated it. It was with a heavy heart that I shelved it.)

Other dishes were triumphant successes. Now at any given time, we have three or four ramen varieties on offer at both restaurants. The dishes at Ivan Ramen Plus are little bit more funky—cheese mazemen and the like. Most of the dishes are unique to the restaurant. In this section are some of our greatest hits—the dishes that I'm most proud of because they're delicious and uniquely mine.

None of these are really easier or quicker alternatives to the shio ramen recipe. Ramen is meant to be eaten quickly, but the good stuff takes time to make. As with the shio ramen, you can pick and choose where you want to cut corners in the following recipes—whether it's using store-bought noodles, substituting katsuobushi for the multiple types of dried fish I call for in the dashi, buying premade stock, or any of the other little shortcuts I offer. On the bright side, a lot of these recipes utilize some of the components of the shio ramen. If you've made extra, you're halfway there.

Roasted Garlic Mazemen

WITH CHICKEN FAT AND CHASU

Mazemen are noodles served with just a little soup; they need to be mixed around in their sauce as they're eaten. They're a bona fide style of ramen, but I'd never heard of them before I came up with them through independent experimentation. During the first few months after opening Ivan Ramen, I was perpetually too busy to construct and eat a full bowl of ramen. But as bundle after bundle of noodles came out of the cooker, I yearned to enjoy the fleeting flavor of freshly cooked pasta. I started quickly mixing a few simple ingredients with noodles fresh out of the cooker, and wolfing them down.

This dish was the first mazemen that made it onto the menu: noodles, a little fat, a little soup, some shio tare, and a big dollop of garlic puree. It's easy and super fast to make and eat (if you have all your ingredients lined up), and the texture of the noodles is better preserved than if they're sitting in a steaming bowl of soup. This is a style I've come to love, and this dish is my go-to family meal.

Makes 1 serving

30 milliliters (2 tablespoons) SHIO TARE (page 107)

10 milliliters (2 teaspoons) CHICKEN FAT (page 104)

10 milliliters (2 teaspoons) garlic oil from ROASTED GARLIC AND GARLIC OIL (page 158)

50 grams (2 ounces) roasted garlic from ROASTED GARLIC AND GARLIC OIL (page 158)

❶ Bring a large pot of unsalted water to a boil for the noodles.

❷ In a ramen bowl, combine the shio tare, chicken fat, garlic oil, garlic puree, and katsuobushi salt. Set aside.

❸ Add the noodles to the pot and cook until just al dente, about 50 seconds. In the meantime, add the hot soup to the ramen bowl and whisk everything thoroughly.

❹ Once they're cooked, drain the noodles thoroughly, shaking them well to get rid of as much water as you can, and drop them into the bowl. **(CONTINUED)**

5 grams (2 teaspoons)
KATSUOBUSHI SALT (page 111)

130 grams (4½ ounces)
TOASTED RYE NOODLES
(page 119) or store-bought
ramen noodles

100 milliliters (½ cup)
DOUBLE SOUP (page 113),
simmering

Thinly sliced green onions

1 (13-millimeter/½-inch)
slice PORK BELLY CHASHU
(page 127), warmed in its
cooking liquid or in the
noodle water as it comes
to a simmer

Aonori (powdered seaweed),
for garnish

(CONTINUED)

5 Mound green onions on top, and casually arrange the piece of chashu nearby. Sprinkle aonori over everything and serve.

6 Give everything a good stir before eating.

Chile Mazemen

WITH EGGPLANT AND CHIPOTLE

This dish was born at the local yaoya, or greengrocer. It was a classic cook's moment, where the ingredients created the dish. Not to sound too hippie, but I was standing at the market, transfixed by a basket of perfect eggplants. I love eggplant, and had seen some places garnish a cold ramen dish with a slice of grilled or pickled eggplant, but I hadn't ever thought to include it in my own ramen. Before I could reason myself out of it, I gathered up the eggplants and headed back to my kitchen.

I decided to toy around with my basic sofrito and replace the garlic, ginger, and apple with onions, eggplant, tomatoes, and chipotle chiles. The resulting sofrito is super creamy with incredible depth of flavor. With a little shoyu tare and the house soup, it became something really unique in Tokyo, and further evidence that letting Mother Nature dictate your menu is good practice.

Once again, please forgive the laundry list of items that you need to produce this dish. I generally find cookbooks that require a lot of special pantry items incredibly annoying, but the resulting dish is worth it, and you can always use components of this ramen in other dishes. Remember to take the chile sofrito out of the fridge in advance; you want it to come to room temperature since you'll be serving it as a topping.

Makes 4 servings

400 milliliters (1½ cups) DOUBLE SOUP (page 113), simmering

40 milliliters (3 tablespoons) CHICKEN FAT (page 104)

120 milliliters (½ cup) SHOYU-SOFRITO TARE (page 166)

520 grams (18 ounces) TOASTED RYE NOODLES (page 119) or store-bought ramen noodles

❶ Bring a large pot of unsalted water to a boil for the noodles.

❷ Set out 4 ramen bowls, and divide the chicken fat and shoyu-sofrito tare evenly among them.

❸ Drop the noodles into the boiling water and cook until they are al dente, about 50 seconds.

❹ About 10 seconds before the noodles are done, ladle the hot soup into the bowls, dividing it evenly. Drain the cooked noodles well, shaking them **(CONTINUED)**

400 milliliters (1½ cups) DOUBLE SOUP (page 113), simmering

320 grams (1¼ cups) room-temperature CHILE SOFRITO (page 167)

4 (13-millimeter/½-inch) slices PORK BELLY CHASHU (page 127), warmed in its cooking liquid or in the noodle water as it comes to a simmer

2 green onions, cut on the bias

Chipotle powder, for garnish

(CONTINUED)

thoroughly to get rid of as much water as you can, and divide among the expectant bowls. Use a pair of chopsticks to mix the noodles with the soup and tare.

5 Divide the chile sofrito among the noodle mounds and lay a piece of chashu on top. Add a heap of green onions and sprinkle chipotle powder over the whole thing. Be sure to mix thoroughly as you eat.

SHOYU-SOFRITO TARE

Use a good quality soy sauce here, or a 50/50 blend of light and dark soy sauces. If you've got a bunch of Ivan Ramen sofrito (page 108) lying around, this is where that hard work pays off.

Makes 1 liter (1 quart)

125 milliliters (½ cup) sake

125 milliliters (½ cup) mirin

350 milliliters (1½ cups) good-quality soy sauce

140 grams (¾ cup) SOFRITO (page 108)

1 Combine the sake and mirin in a small saucepan, bring it up to a simmer over medium heat, and let the alcohol cook off for 3 minutes. Add the soy sauce and bring back to a simmer, then stir in the sofrito.

2 Turn off the heat and let cool to room temperature. Store in the refrigerator for up to 2 weeks.

CHILE SOFRITO

I love this recipe because it shows how we create new dishes at the restaurant while staying within the same basic structure. Just like the sofrito in our shio ramen, this chile sofrito forms a base upon which other flavors can be layered. This sofrito is very savory and a little bit spicy. It speaks to the way we should all cook—letting what's available locally dictate what we make, rather than coming up with an idea and then going out of our way to make it happen.

Makes about 1 liter (1 quart)

500 milliliters (2 cups) vegetable oil

350 grams (12 ounces) onions, diced small

150 grams (5 ounces) eggplant, diced small

250 grams (9 ounces) tomatoes, diced small

9 grams (2½ teaspoons) chipotle powder

1 Combine the oil, onions, and eggplant in a large saucepan set over the lowest possible heat; if you have a heat diffuser, use it. Cook for 4 hours, stirring regularly. The oil should bubble lightly, not simmer; you want the vegetables to soften and melt but not really brown. After 4 hours, add the tomatoes and continue to cook for 1 more hour. Finally, add the chipotle powder and cook for 1 more hour. The oil will take on a deep-red hue, and the vegetables should be soft, almost to the point of falling apart.

2 Cool to room temperature and store, sealed, in the refrigerator. The sofrito should last at least a week, likely two.

Toasted Sesame and Spicy Chile Tsukemen

WITH FAT RYE NOODLES

Tsukemen **is a type of ramen** modeled after its more illustrious cousin, soba (buckwheat noodles). Soba is the most Japanese of Japanese noodles, and it's most commonly served cold with a side of soy-flavored dashi (also cold). Tsukemen is different from soba in that, while the noodles are cold, the broth is hot. Since the broth is meant to be consumed as a dipping sauce and not as a soup (although some places will add a little hot soup to your dip at the end and encourage you to drink it), it's much more pungent and intense than normal ramen broth. Tsukemen was invented by Kazuo Yamagishi, the owner of Taishoken, one of the more legendary ramen shops in Tokyo. In the last four or five years, tsukemen has taken Japan by storm—there are now shops that peddle tsukemen exclusively.

When I opened Ivan Ramen, I wasn't a big fan of tsukemen, but I felt compelled to accommodate its popularity. But my tsukemen never quite came together the way I wanted, and I took it off the menu after a few months. The following year, I went back to the drawing board. I realized that the real joy of tsukemen is that it highlights the noodle. Around the time I started trying again, my flour purveyor sent me a bag of rye flour. Rye is a really interesting flour—incredibly fragrant, and with much less gluten than wheat. Of course, it also immediately sent me back to my Jewish childhood, when my mother would buy a fresh loaf of rye bread every Friday for Shabbos.

At this point, I didn't know anybody who used whole grain flours in ramen noodles. When I told people I wanted to use rye in my noodles, they warned me not to make a noodle with flecks of grain in it—"People will think it's bugs or dirt." But the rye gives the noodles a beautiful aroma and more integrity. Five years later, whole grain noodles are everywhere. I'm not suggesting I started the trend, I'm just saying . . .

(CONTINUED)

Makes 4 servings

150 grams (1¼ cups) toasted sesame seeds

10 grams (1½ tablespoons) crushed red chile flakes

14 grams (2½ tablespoons) KATSUOBUSHI SALT (page 111)

110 grams (4 ounces) roasted garlic from ROASTED GARLIC AND GARLIC OIL (page 158)

60 milliliters (¼ cup) rice vinegar

45 grams (2 tablespoons) honey

225 milliliters (1 cup) SHOYU-SOFRITO TARE (page 166)

40 milliliters (3 tablespoons) PORK FAT (page 105)

560 milliliters (1½ cups) DOUBLE SOUP (page 113), simmering

800 grams (1¾ pounds) FAT RYE NOODLES, cooked and chilled (page 171)

4 thick slices PORK BELLY CHASHU (page 127), warmed in its cooking liquid or in the noodle water as it comes to a simmer

Sliced green onions or negi (Japanese green onions), for garnish

4 HALF-COOKED EGGS (page 131), optional

(CONTINUED)

1 Grind the sesame seeds and chile flakes in a mortar and pestle until they're about half the size they started. (Alternatively, you can do this in a food processor, but pulse carefully or you'll end up with butter.)

2 Mix the ground seeds and chile with the katsuobushi salt, pureed garlic, vinegar, honey, and shoyu-sofrito tare. Set out 4 cups or bowls and divide the mixture among them, then divvy up the pork fat.

3 Distribute the hot soup among the cups or bowls. Whisk each briefly to combine everything.

4 Pile the chilled noodles onto 4 separate plates and set a piece of warm chashu on top of each pile. Sprinkle with green onions. Nestle a halved half-cooked egg on the plate, if you're using them.

5 To eat, dip some noodles into the soup and slurp them up.

FAT RYE NOODLES

This recipe is a bit difficult to translate to the home kitchen. Flour and water are different all over the country, and very different from what's available in Japan. Ramen dough is odd—not quite wet and not quite dry—and doesn't easily come together. Having said that, making your own noodles is rewarding, and you'll only get better with practice. God knows my first fifty batches of noodles were made with little to no knowledge, and on a hand-cranked pasta machine. If I could do it, you certainly can.

Makes about 1 kilo (2 pounds)

70 grams (½ cup) rye flour

620 grams (4 cups) cake flour

300 grams (2 cups) high-gluten (14 to 15 percent protein) bread flour

10 grams (1½ teaspoons) kansui powder (see note, page 119)

430 milliliters (1¾ cups) water

13 grams (1 tablespoon) salt

Cornstarch

❶ In the bowl of a stand mixer, combine the flours and set aside.

❷ In a separate bowl, slowly stir the kansui into the water until it's fully dissolved (this takes a little time). Then stir in the salt to dissolve.

❸ Outfit your mixer with the dough hook attachment. With the mixer running on low speed, add the water in thirds to the flour mixture. After a few minutes, the dough should begin to come together. It will be a bit shaggy—more so than Italian pasta dough. If it isn't coming together at all, add a spoonful of water. Once it comes together, increase the speed to medium-low and let the machine run for 10 minutes, until the dough forms a ball. Turn off the mixer and cover the dough with plastic wrap. Let stand for 30 minutes.

❹ After 30 minutes, the dough should be significantly softer in texture and smoother in appearance. Set the dough ball on a cutting board, flatten it with the palm of your hand, then cut it into four 5-centimeter (2-inch) strips. Cover the dough strips with a damp kitchen towel.

❺ Set up your pasta machine and adjust it to the largest size. Pass one sheet of dough through the machine, then fold it over on itself so that you have a double sheet. Turn the machine to the second largest size, and run the doubled sheet through. Double the sheet over again, and run it through the third largest setting. **(CONTINUED)**

(CONTINUED)

6 Don't double the sheet over again. Run it through the fourth largest setting, then once through the smallest setting. Set aside and repeat with the remaining sheets of dough. Once the dough is all rolled, pass the sheets through the widest cutter you have, or cut by hand into fettuccine-width noodles. You should have a nice, wide noodle with a little heft. Toss the noodles with a little cornstarch to keep them from sticking together, and shake off the excess before cooking. Store the noodles in a container wrapped tightly with plastic (or individual portions in ziplock bags) for up to a day.

7 Cook the noodles until just al dente in a large pot of boiling unsalted water; this will probably take 2½ to 3 minutes, but the first time you make this, you'll need to watch and test them to find the right timing.

8 Once the noodles are cooked, drain them and run them under cold water, stirring with your hand to completely cool them. Shake them thoroughly in the strainer to get rid of as much water as possible before serving.

Four-Cheese Mazemen

EDAM, PARMESAN, MOZZARELLA, AND MONTEREY JACK

This is the signature dish at Ivan Ramen Plus, my second shop. Cheese is continuing to find its way into more and more bowls of ramen, but it's still not the most common ingredient. "Fusion" is a no-no word these days, but I love combining Western and Japanese ingredients and sensibilities. This bowl has Edam and Parmesan cheese and lemon, but also dashi, katsuobushi, and pickled bean sprouts. And while this dish is cheesy, it's also balanced. The four-cheese mazemen is still hands down the most popular dish on the menu.

The tricky part of this dish is making sure that the cheese completely melts into the soup. In addition to the Edam and Parmesan, there's also inexpensive melty cheese from Hokkaido (it's Monterey Jack, basically) and mozzarella. If you can't find fish powder, you could substitute a pile of katsuobushi or even sprinkle some crumbled bacon instead. I may sound like a broken record, but when you make these dishes at home, just remember to taste and use your imagination; be willing to adjust if it doesn't taste exactly how you like. I'm giving you the recipes as we make them, but the differences in ingredients can be limiting, so stretch where you need to. Maybe you'll come up with something better.

Makes 4 servings

500 grams (1 pound) very fresh bean sprouts, the fatter the better

500 milliliters (2 cups) water

100 milliliters (½ cup) rice vinegar

1 clove garlic

65 grams (¼ cup) sugar

1 Rinse the bean sprouts under cold water. Shake off the excess water and place them in a heatproof bowl.

2 In a small saucepan, mix the water, vinegar, and garlic, and bring to a simmer. Add the sugar and stir until it's dissolved. Pour the hot vinegar mixture over the bean sprouts and let cool to room temperature. Refrigerate the bean sprouts in the liquid until ready to use. They should hold for about a week. **(CONTINUED)**

200 milliliters (¾ cup) AGO DASHI (page 179) or regular DASHI (page 116)

100 grams (3½ ounces) shredded mozzarella

100 grams (3½ ounces) shredded Monterey Jack

120 milliliters (1½ cup) SHIO TARE (page 107)

Juice of 1 lemon

Zest of 2 lemons

720 grams (1½ pounds) FAT RYE NOODLES (page 171)

60 grams (2 ounces) grated Edam

60 grams (2 ounces) grated Parmesan

12 grams (2 tablespoons) katsuobushi (bonito) powder (see page 111, steps 1 and 2)

4 grams (1 teaspoon) sea salt

4 thick slices PORK BELLY CHASHU (page 127), warmed in its cooking liquid or in the noodle water as it comes to a simmer

2 room-temperature HALF-COOKED EGGS (page 131), sliced in half

Finely chopped chives

(CONTINUED)

❸ Bring a large pot of unsalted water to a boil for the noodles. Bring the dashi to a simmer in a small saucepan.

❹ Set out 4 ramen bowls. Although it's a bit of a pain to warm the bowls, it helps the cheese melt. To warm them, bring about 7.5 centimeters (3 inches) of water to a simmer in a shallow pan. Place the bowls in the water one at a time, spinning and turning it until it's warm, then remove it from the water. Divide the mozzarella, Monterey Jack, shio tare, lemon juice, and lemon zest among the warmed bowls.

❺ Drop the noodles into the boiling water and cook until just past al dente, about 3 minutes. About 10 seconds before the noodles are ready, divide the hot dashi among the bowls.

❻ Drain the noodles thoroughly, shaking the strainer up and down and from side to side to get rid of as much water as you can, and divvy them up. Use a pair of chopsticks to thoroughly mix the noodles, dashi, and cheese. The hot noodles should help the cheese melt.

❼ Sprinkle the Edam, Parmesan, katsuobushi, and sea salt over each bowl. Place a piece of warm chashu in the center of each bowl, nestle half an egg into the noodles, and top with a heap of pickled bean sprouts and a sprinkling of chives. Give everything a good stir and eat quickly, before the cheese cools and firms back up.

Ago Dashi Ramen

WITH SHOYU TARE

Ivan Ramen Plus is all about dashi. Since first moving to Japan, I've been enamored of dashi and fascinated by the notion of making a fish-based soup with as much umami as a meat broth, or even more. I've experimented with dozens of dried and smoked fish, as well as shellfish and all sorts of konbu. (In fact, the menu at Ivan Ramen Plus was originally based entirely around fish soups—no meat or poultry.)

Ago, or flying fish, is sweeter and doesn't have the bitter edge of iriko (sardine) that most ramen shops use in their dashis. It's a bit more common in southern Japan, but it's also quite expensive. But if you're going to make fish the star of the show, you ought to use the best fish, so I went for it, and I don't regret it for a second. If you can't find it, use katsuobushi (bonito). This ago soup is sweet, aromatic, rich, and strong enough to provide the backbone for a bowl of ramen.

Makes 4 servings

4 halves SLOW-ROASTED TOMATOES (page 195)

50 milliliters (3½ tablespoons) garlic oil from ROASTED GARLIC AND GARLIC OIL (page 158)

1.1 liters (4¾ cups) AGO DASHI (page 179)

120 milliliters (½ cup) SHOYU TARE (page 180)

40 milliliters (3 tablespoons) CHICKEN FAT (page 104)

1 Puree the tomatoes and garlic oil in a food processor and set aside.

2 Boil a large pot of unsalted water for the noodles. In a separate saucepan, bring the dashi to a simmer.

3 Set out 4 ramen bowls. Divide the shoyu tare and chicken fat among the bowls.

4 Drop the noodles into the boiling water and cook for about 50 seconds, until the noodles are just past al dente. About 10 seconds before they're done, divide the hot dashi among the bowls. **(CONTINUED)**

520 grams (18 ounces)
TOASTED RYE NOODLES
(page 119)

4 fat slices PORK BELLY
CHASHU (page 127), warmed
in its cooking liquid or in the
noodle water as it comes to
a simmer

12 strips MENMA (page 123)

12 grams (2 tablespoons)
ago (flying fish) powder or
katsuobushi (bonito) powder
(see page 111, steps 1 and 2)

20 grams (¾ ounce) grated
Parmesan

A small pile of mizuna leaves
for each bowl

(CONTINUED)

Drain the noodles thoroughly, shaking the strainer well to
get rid of as much water as possible. Divide the noodles
among the bowls. Lift them with a pair of chopsticks or
tongs and fold them back over themselves, so that they
don't clump into a ball.

5 Lay a piece of chashu on top of the noodles, then 4 strips
of menma and a spoonful of tomato puree. Sprinkle fish
powder and Parmesan over everything and finish with a
small nest of mizuna in the center. Serve immediately.

AGO DASHI

An accurate thermometer is essential to making ago dashi. The ingredients are delicate and break down very quickly if the temperature gets too high. You'll also want a fine-mesh skimmer, china cap, or colander lined with cheesecloth. The dashi can produce a lot of sediment, and the konbu gives off a gooey slick that should be skimmed off.

Makes about 2 liters (2 quarts)

2 liters (2 quarts) cold water

60 grams (2 ounces) ago (dried flying fish)

40 grams (1½ ounces) geso (dried squid tentacles)

20 grams (¾ ounce) ebi (dried shrimp)

20 grams (¾ ounce) kaibashira (dried scallops)

30 grams (1 ounce) konbu

60 grams (2 ounces) katsuobushi (shaved dried bonito), or a premixed blend of shaved dried mackerel, sardine, and bonito, if you can find it

1 In a pot, combine the water with the ago, geso, ebi, kaibashira, and konbu, and let soak for at least 2 hours, or overnight, in the fridge.

2 With a fine-mesh skimmer, scoop off any slime released by the konbu. Set the pot of soaked ingredients over medium heat and heat the liquid to 140°F (60°C). Turn off the heat and immediately strain the soup through a fine-mesh strainer, china cap, or a cheesecloth-lined collander, being sure to allow all of the liquid to drain from the ingredients.

3 Put the liquid back in the pot and return it to the stove. Over medium-high heat, bring it to 176°F (80°C) and add the katsuobushi. Lower the heat, and keep the temperature at 176°F (80°C) for 5 minutes, then strain the dashi again. Use immediately or chill and store; it will keep for a couple days in the refrigerator.

SHOYU TARE

Shoyu tare is made with soy sauce as a base. It's the seasoning for shoyu ramen, and it's used in a few other variations introduced later in the book. There's no question that the quality of the soy sauce you use is important. If you don't have konbu powder, use dried sheets cut into small pieces or pulverized in a blender.

You'll notice that I'm very specific about the temperature at which this should be cooked. The flavors in dried seafood are very delicate and will break down rapidly and even turn bitter if the temperature gets too high. Decades of experimentation by Japanese cooks has determined that 176°F (80°C) is the sweet spot for making dashi and tare. Any type of instant-read thermometer will make this procedure simple to follow. But having said that, no one's life will be ruined if you just wing it. Just don't let the liquid boil—a bare simmer is okay.

Makes 300 milliliters (1¼ cups)

50 milliliters (3½ tablespoons) sake

50 milliliters (3½ tablespoons) mirin

100 milliliters (½ cup + 1 tablespoon) usukuchi (light) soy sauce

100 milliliters (½ cup + 1 tablespoon) koikuchi (dark) soy sauce

2 grams (a 1-inch square) konbu

3 kaibashira (dried scallops)

10 grams (⅓ ounce) sababushi (shaved dried mackerel) or katsuobushi (shaved dried bonito)

❶ In a small saucepan, bring the sake and mirin to a simmer over medium-high heat and cook off the alcohol for 3 minutes.

❷ Add the soy sauces and bring to 176°F (80°C) over medium-high heat. The mixture shouldn't be simmering or even bubbling. The liquid will be too hot for you to hold your finger in for more than about a second.

❸ Add the konbu, kaibashira, and sababushi. Stir and maintain the temperature at 176°F (80°C) for 10 minutes.

❹ Turn off the heat and let the shoyu tare come to room temperature. Strain and use immediately, or store in an airtight container in the refrigerator. It will keep for at least a week.

Ago Tsukemen

WITH ROASTED GARLIC

I created this dish for a pop-up dinner in Atlanta. It was the first time I'd ever done a multicourse ramen dinner. The whole point of ramen is to provide a complete meal in a bowl. The idea of offering more than one ramen dish presented the challenge of creating several different noodle experiences without overstuffing the diners.

This dish is served cold, like soba, with a cold ago-based soup. I haven't tried this in Japan, but my American customers immediately see the playfulness of it and the parallels to soba. I think customers in Tokyo would find it a little sacrilegious and beside the point, partly because there's so much good soba available everywhere. Oh well.

Makes 4 servings

520 grams (18 ounces)
TOASTED RYE NOODLES
(page 119)

200 milliliters (¾ cup) chilled
AGO DASHI (page 179)

8 grams (1 teaspoon) roasted
garlic from ROASTED GARLIC
AND GARLIC OIL (page 158)

12 milliliters (2½ teaspoons)
garlic oil from ROASTED
GARLIC AND GARLIC OIL
(page 158)

8 grams (1½ tablespoons)
KATSUOBUSHI SALT (page 111)

80 milliliters (5½ tablespoons)
SHOYU-SOFRITO TARE
(page 166)

1. Bring a large pot of unsalted water to a boil for the noodles. Cook the noodles until just past al dente, about 50 seconds. Plunge them immediately into an ice bath to stop the cooking. When the noodles are chilled, drain them thoroughly, shaking the strainer up and down and from side to side to get out as much water as you can. Divide them among 4 chilled plates.

2. Combine and mix the dashi, garlic puree, garlic oil, katsuobushi salt, and tare in a large bowl. Divide the mixture among 4 cups and serve alongside the noodles. To eat, dip the noodles in the soup and slurp up.

Breakfast Yakisoba

WITH CHASHU AND EGGS

When I returned to New York to open a branch of Ivan Ramen stateside, I was overwhelmed by the enthusiasm and support from the chef community here. Everyone was eager to help me find contractors and realtors, warn me away from legendarily bad locations, and open their kitchens for me to do pop-ups. One of those pop-up opportunities came from chef April Bloomfield at The Breslin. Together, we put together a "nose to tail" ramen event: she butchered a pig and I created dishes making use of the different cuts.

One of my favorite touches was our take-home goody bag. For years, fancy restaurants have given their diners granola or muffins for breakfast the next morning. I thought it'd be funny to send everyone home with breakfast yakisoba (stir-fried noodles). Everyone got little vacuum packs of noodles, sauce, and chashu, along with instructions on how to cook them. This recipe is a version of those goody-bag noodles. You can use any fresh Asian noodles, but Chinese markets usually offer fresh chow mein–style egg noodles that are ideal for yakisoba. If you don't want to make chashu, a couple strips of bacon will work just fine, too. Breakfast of champions!

Makes 2 servings

250 milliliters (1 cup) water

2 grams (a 1-inch square) konbu

3 kaibashira (dried scallops)

1 dried shiitake mushroom

25 milliliters (2 tablespoons) sake

1 In a bowl, combine the water, konbu, kaibashira, and shiitake, and allow to rehydrate for at least 1½ hours, or overnight, in the refrigerator.

2 To make the tare, combine the sake and mirin in a small saucepan over medium heat and bring to a simmer. Cook for 3 minutes, then add the soaked konbu, kaibashira, shiitake, along with the soaking liquid and bring to 176°F (80°C); the liquid won't simmer, but will be too hot for you to hold your finger in for more than a second. **(CONTINUED)**

25 milliliters (2 tablespoons) mirin

5 grams (¼ ounce) sababushi (shaved dried mackerel), or substitute katsuobushi (shaved dried bonito)

5 grams (1¼ teaspoons) sea salt

1 medium onion, sliced

Vegetable oil

2 cloves garlic, smashed and minced

150 grams (2 cups) shredded green cabbage

3 medium carrots, peeled and grated

2 large eggs

300 grams (10½ ounces) fresh Asian noodles (see note, page 183)

4 thick slices PORK BELLY CHASHU (page 127), warmed in its cooking liquid or in the noodle water as it comes to a simmer

(CONTINUED)

Keep at this temperature for 10 minutes, then add the sababushi and hold at 176°F (80°C) for 5 minutes more. Strain out the solids and add the salt to the tare, stirring until it's fully dissolved. Reserve until needed. You can make this the night before and keep it in the fridge if you have the foresight.

3 Bring a pot of unsalted water to a boil for the noodles.

4 While the water is heating, sauté the onion in an oiled pan over medium-high heat until it just begins to caramelize— about 7 minutes. Add the garlic and cook for 3 minutes, then add the cabbage and carrots and cook until tender, about another 10 minutes. Reserve.

5 In a small nonstick skillet, fry your eggs how you like them. I like my yolks runny. Set them aside.

6 Cook the noodles until al dente, 2½ to 3 minutes. Drain very thoroughly, add the noodles to a lightly oiled non-stick skillet over high heat, and cook until slightly crispy, about 5 minutes. Add the vegetables and stir everything together with chopsticks. Add the tare and continue to cook and stir for 3 more minutes.

7 Divide the noodles between 2 plates and top with the chashu and eggs. That's an Ivan Ramen breakfast!

Bacon, Lettuce, and Tomato Mazemen

IVAN RAMEN SUMMER SPECIAL

This is a special dish I run regularly in the spring and summer, and it is always popular. The Japanese love tomatoes, even if they are expensive as hell. The BLT is popular in Tokyo, but I've never really had a great one there, because the bacon sucks. (I always look forward to a big pile of bacon when I come back to New York.) This dish was the first one I created upon returning to the States. It has all the elements of a classic BLT, with a smoky, fishy twist and, of course, noodles. Plus, it's a great chance to use some of the different components you've made for Ivan Ramen shio ramen.

Makes 4 servings

175 grams (1 cup) mayonnaise

30 milliliters (2 tablespoons) DASHI (page 116)

15 milliliters (1 tablespoon) SHIO TARE (page 107)

15 milliliters (1 tablespoon) lemon juice

Zest of 1 lemon

520 grams (18 ounces) TOASTED RYE NOODLES (page 119) or store-bought ramen noodles

① Bring a large pot of unsalted water to a boil for the noodles.

② In a small bowl, combine the mayonnaise, dashi, shio tare, lemon juice, and lemon zest. Set aside.

③ Cook the noodles until they're a little past al dente, about a minute. (Because these noodles will be served chilled, you should cook them a touch softer than you would if they were being served hot. There'll be no hot soup to continue cooking them, and the noodles will firm a bit when chilled.) As soon as they're cooked, plunge them into an ice bath to chill them, then drain them thoroughly, shaking the strainer well to get rid of as much water as possible. **(CONTINUED)**

4 thick slices ripe tomato

4 halves SLOW-ROASTED TOMATOES (page 195)

1 head iceberg lettuce, cut into 4 wedges

12 slices thick-cut good-quality bacon, cooked crisp

Sea salt and pepper

Katsuobushi (shaved dried bonito)

(CONTINUED)

4 In a large mixing bowl, toss the noodles with three-quarters of the mayo-tare mixture until the noodles are well coated.

5 Divide the dressed noodles among 4 chilled ramen bowls and arrange the two types of tomatoes and the wedges of iceberg lettuce and bacon on top. Drizzle the remaining mayo-tare mixture over the top, sprinkle with salt and pepper, and finish with a small handful of katsuobushi.

Sides and Sweets

When I opened Ivan Ramen, I felt strongly that my customers should get a real, full dining experience. Too often I've gone for a bowl of ramen and been done with my bowl after seven or eight minutes, and felt like I hadn't even gone out to eat yet.

Likewise, you may find it anticlimactic to spend days preparing Ivan Ramen from scratch, only to have your guests slurp it down in a few minutes and look at you as if to say, "That's it?" A few side dishes can make the occasion a little more festive and draw out a good experience a little longer.

Most ramen shops have a very limited side menu if they have one at all—usually just gyoza (aka potstickers) and maybe some dishes consisting of leftover chashu chopped up in rice and doused with a sweet soy-based sauce. Some places chop up negi (Japanese green onions), mix it with sesame oil and salt, and serve it over rice. I wanted something both a little more substantial and a little more unique.

What I came up with were a couple of different rice bowls based around two simple toppings: roasted tomato and pork. The pork is different from the chashu we serve with our noodles. It's slow-cooked, then shredded, and it's the basis for two pork-crazy side dishes in this chapter—one that I've been serving at Ivan Ramen Tokyo forever, and one I developed for Ivan Ramen New York.

As for sweets, the very few ramen shops that serve dessert might offer almond tofu or pudding from a mix—nothing memorable. I really felt that I needed to offer dessert for a complete dining experience. I got an ice cream maker and started tinkering. I discovered that the problem is that it's hard to taste certain flavors after all that salt and fat. I made a delicious chocolate sorbet that tasted fantastic on its own, but after a bowl of ramen, the subtleties of the chocolate just vanished—everything was muted. I needed something tart and refreshing. Inspired by a David Lebovitz recipe, I landed on lemon sherbet. With a little salt and a lot of lemon, I ended up with a dessert that was the perfect foil to a bowl of ramen and also happened to really fit the flavor profile Japanese people love: sour, salty, and only mildly sweet. The sherbet cuts through the salt and fat taste left on your palate after slurping a bowl of ramen, but it still has the creamy mouthfeel of ice cream. We've toyed around with a few different flavors through the years, but this one always stays on the menu.

Steamed Rice

A BASIC RECIPE

If you have a rice cooker, more power to you. I have the latest, greatest nanotechnology rocket-ship doohickey that makes super fantastic special rice, but you can make it the traditional way, too. A cup of uncooked white rice will yield about 2 cups of cooked rice.

Makes as much as you want

1 part Japanese short-grain white rice

1 part water

❶ Rinse the rice several times under cool water until the water runs clear. Drain the rice well.

❷ Combine the rice and the water in a heavy-bottomed saucepan. Bring to a simmer over medium heat. Cover, turn the heat down to low, and cook for 18 minutes—no need to add fat or salt.

❸ Uncover and fluff with a fork. Leftover rice can be wrapped in plastic and frozen in small portions.

Pork and Tomato Meshi

STEAMED RICE BOWLS WITH TOPPINGS

When I first started coming up with side dishes for my shop, I thought of roasted tomatoes. I had been roasting tomatoes at work and at home for years—slicing them in half, sprinkling them with oil, salt, and pepper, and popping them in a low oven until they become semidried, chewy flavor bombs. I'd served them in every conceivable way: on toast, in pasta, as steak garnish, or with slices of mozzarella cheese. I figured, why not serve them on rice? Tomatoes are loaded with umami, which would fit with everything else in my umami-overloaded ramen shop.

This is really two recipes in one. We serve the roasted tomatoes alone with rice; same with the pork shoulder. But the best way to eat this is as one combined dish. I'm proud to say that that dish has graced the covers of magazines in Japan. (Of course, if you're serving fatty pulled pork with slow-roasted tomatoes, and people don't love it, you're doing something wrong.)

These side dishes are known as meshi—small rice bowls—but there are endless other ways to utilize the tomatoes and pork shoulder. Always make more tomatoes than you need; submerged in olive oil, they'll hold for a few weeks. Fatty pork freezes well and can be used to goose up tomato sauce or make awesome sliders.

Makes 4 servings

720 grams (4 cups) warm
STEAMED RICE (page 191)

Warm SHREDDED FATTY
PORK (page 194)

SLOW-ROASTED TOMATOES
(page 195)

Green onions or negi
(Japanese green onions),
sliced, for garnish

1 Spoon 1 cup of the warm rice into each of 4 bowls and flatten it down.

2 Top with a generous helping of pork. No rice should be visible. Stack 2 roasted tomato halves on top of each serving. Garnish with green onions for crunch.

SHREDDED FATTY PORK

Makes 795 grams (1¾ pounds)

1 (140 grams/3-pound) piece of boneless, skinless pork shoulder

8 cloves garlic, peeled

Salt and pepper

❶ Preheat the oven to 250°F (120°C). Cut the pork shoulder into roughly 5-centimeter (2-inch) chunks and place them in a roasting pan that can hold all the meat in one layer while leaving a bit of room around each piece. Add enough water to come one-third of the way up the sides the meat pieces. Toss in the garlic and sprinkle everything with 1 teaspoon salt and ½ teaspoon pepper.

❷ Cover the roasting pan tightly with plastic wrap and then with foil. Put the pan in the oven and leave it alone for 2 hours. The plastic wrap creates a tight seal that efficiently traps in the heat. Don't mess with the seal. After 2 hours, check the meat every 30 minutes or so. When it falls apart when pressed with a fork, it's done.

❸ Remove the meat and garlic cloves to a bowl and smash with a fork until the pork is shredded and the garlic is well incorporated. Add in spoonfuls of cooking liquid to moisten the meat to your liking. Season to taste with salt.

SLOW-ROASTED TOMATOES

Makes 8 tomato halves

4 medium or large tomatoes (or more)

Vegetable oil

Salt and pepper

❶ Preheat the oven to 225°F (110°C). Slice the tomatoes in half and core them. Place them cut side up on a sheet tray, brush them lightly with oil, and sprinkle with salt and pepper.

❷ Put the tomatoes in the oven and cook until shriveled but still juicy looking. This should take about 3 hours, but it'll depend on the tomatoes, so be patient and check regularly after the first 2½ hours. You're looking for the tomatoes to be soft and a little leathery, but still moist.

Roasted Pork Musubi

WITH PICKLED PLUM AND ROASTED TOMATO

This is my homage to the pork bun. David Chang, God bless him, took a Chinatown staple (the roast duck bun), added pork, and put it on his menu at Momofuku to incredible acclaim. It deserves all the praise it gets—it's delicious. But now it's on every ramen shop menu in America. What Dave did with the bun is to me the essence of good noodle-shop business. The noodles are the heart and soul of the restaurant, but nothing beats having a solid appetizer that every person just has to order with their noodles.

When I began planning the menu for my New York restaurant, I came up with this humble answer to the pork bun. It's a riff on musubi, a seasoned Japanese rice ball. A little scoop of rice goes on a triangle of toasted nori, then is topped with a pile of warm fatty pork, wasabi, and umeboshi (pickled plum). (When buying umeboshi, look for the larger, softer ones, and avoid the hard, small, dark red ones.) It looks like a piece of pork sushi. I doubt people would bang down the door to order "pork sushi," though.

Makes 4 small servings

4 medium-sized umeboshi

15 to 30 milliliters (1 to 2 tablespoons) wasabi paste (from a tube is fine)

Honey, optional

1 sheet nori

135 grams (¾ cup) warm STEAMED RICE (page 191)

❶ Remove the pits from the umeboshi and chop the flesh finely. Add to a small mixing bowl and add an equivalent amount of wasabi paste. Mix together thoroughly. If the resulting paste is too spicy for your liking, add ¼ to ½ teaspoon of honey to the mix.

❷ Quickly pass the nori sheet back and forth about 6 inches above an open flame or a hot gas burner. Use tongs if you're afraid of burning your hands, but don't let the sheet linger. You just want to wave it over the heat so that it gets a tiny bit crisp. Nori burns easily, so be careful. Cut the toasted sheet into quarters, then cut each quarter in half diagonally, resulting in 8 small triangles. Lay out the pieces on a platter. **(CONTINUED)**

170 grams (¾ cup)
SHREDDED FATTY PORK
(page 194)

2 halves SLOW-ROASTED
TOMATOES (page 195), each
half cut into 4 pieces

(CONTINUED)

3 Scoop up rice with a round spoon and nestle a mound (about a golf ball's worth) onto each nori triangle. Divide the pork among the rice balls.

4 Carefully top the pork with wasabi-umeboshi paste and a piece of tomato. You can fold the points of the nori triangle up to mimic a little piece of sushi, or just leave them flat for your diners to fold up and devour.

Lemon Sherbet

WITH A TOUCH OF SALT

I'll be quite plain: this sherbet kicks ass. It's a good balance of sweet, sour, and salty. And while it might not be the best thing to eat on the boardwalk at Coney Island, it's perfect for dissolving some of the fat left on your palate after a hefty bowl of ramen. It surprises everyone, and has gotten much more attention than I ever thought it would. Something about simple things, I guess.

Makes 1 liter (1 quart)

100 grams (½ cup) sugar

Zest of 2 lemons

300 milliliters (1¼ cups) whole milk

300 milliliters (1¼ cups) heavy cream

150 milliliters (⅔ cup) lemon juice

7 grams (2 teaspoons) kosher salt

1 In a food processor, process the sugar and lemon zest together until the sugar takes on a yellow hue.

2 In a mixing bowl, whisk together the milk and cream, then stir in the lemon sugar until it dissolves. Stir in the lemon juice, then the salt. Mix until the salt is fully dissolved, about a minute.

3 Churn the mixture in your ice cream maker according to the manufacturer's instructions.

4 Let the sherbet fully set in the freezer for at least an hour or two before you eat it.

Tomato Sorbet

WITH SLOW-ROASTED TOMATOES

Massoud was an Iranian cook who worked for us at Ivan Ramen for two years. He's lived in Tokyo for the better part of twenty years, and is effectively Japanese. When I wasn't in the shop, everyone assumed he was me, because, you know, all foreigners look alike. After a while, we stopped correcting them. Anyway, he came up with this sorbet as a special, and it quickly became a hit. I assure you it doesn't just taste like frozen tomatoes with sugar.

Makes 1 liter (1 quart)

Zest of 2 lemons

120 grams (½ cup) sugar

4 medium-sized ripe tomatoes, peeled, seeded, and chopped

4 halves SLOW-ROASTED TOMATOES (page 195)

150 milliliters (⅔ cup) lemon juice

7 grams (2 teaspoons) kosher salt

1 In a food processor, process the sugar and zest together until the sugar takes on a yellow hue.

2 Puree both the fresh and roasted tomatoes with a hand blender or in a food processor until smooth. Add the lemon sugar and continue to puree until the sugar is completely dissolved. Stir in the lemon juice, then the salt, blending until the salt dissolves.

3 Churn the mixture in your ice cream maker according to the manufacturer's instructions.

4 Let the sorbet fully set in the freezer for at least an hour or two before you eat it.

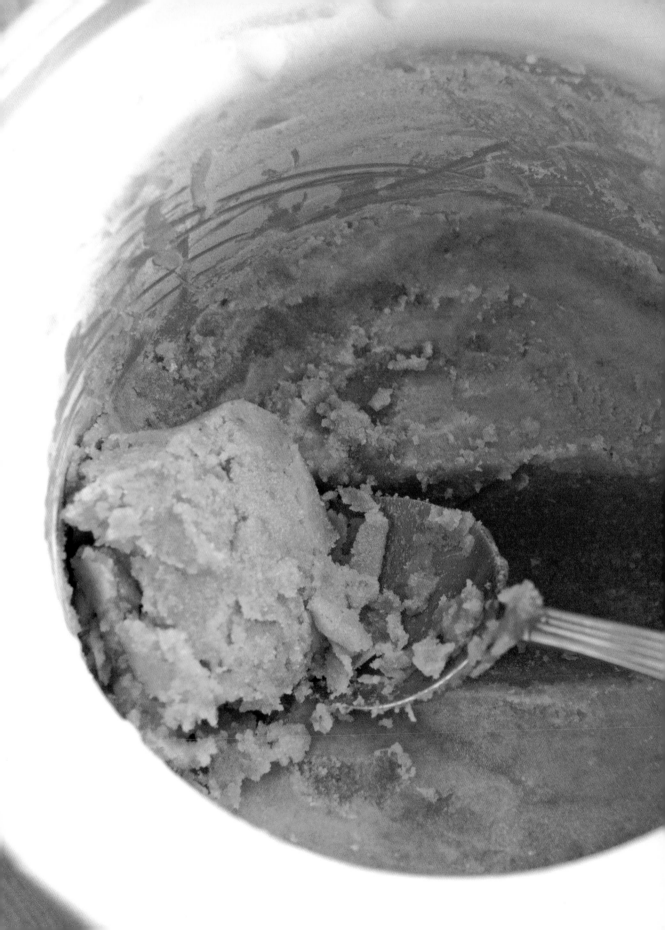

Acknowledgments

How do you give thanks for forty-nine years of success and failure, and to whom? So many people have been there for me throughout the years, and who reads these things anyway?

Endless gratitude to my wife Mari, who was the only person to ever look me square in the eye and say, "You will succeed at anything you do!" I had no idea what she was talking about, but as usual in our very successful marriage, I did whatever she told me to do. What can I say? I'm a good Jewish husband.

Thanks and love to:

My boys Isaac, Alex, and Ren, who give me constant joy and purpose.

My mom, whose strength since my dad's death has been inspiring to all of us. Thank you for not returning me to wherever I came from in those turbulent childhood years.

My sisters Jenny and Tricia and my brothers-in-law Ken and Marc. Thank you for being there for me over and over again, through death and birth, and thank you for finding me a house. What a great family to be a part of.

The Kaplans, Aunt Alice, Seth, Isabel, and Caroline, who are as close to me now as ever. Uncle Alan, you're sorely missed.

David and Leslie, for supporting me through everything, with David during the darkest days, to the first Ivan Ramen, and the creation of Ivan Ramen New York.

Taro and Shochan for making Ivan Ramen possible.

My neighbors in Rokakoen. How wonderful to be treated like family.

All my customers, who gave Ivan Ramen a chance.

Shimamoto-san for teaching me how to make noodles.

Shimazaki-san for showing me how it's done.

Matsumoto-san, who runs my restaurants like they were his own.

Ken, Naka, and George at Sun Noodle, who share my vision.

The whole crew at Ivan Ramen and Ivan Ramen Plus, who always make me look good.

Mike, Jeff, Marcelo, Doug, Peter, Danny, and Marci, my high-school chums who always had faith in me.

Eric and Ayako, who took me in when all seemed lost and have always been there since.

Kim Witherspoon for believing in my story.

David Chang and Peter Meehan for taking me seriously.

Noriko for taking awesome pictures.

Daniel Krieger for handling the New York photos and doing it with his usual style.

Gregory Starr for getting Kodansha to do the original book project.

Ted, Ako, Max, and Amy—my first "常連さん."

What does "with Chris Ying" mean anyway?

When I think of Chris, I imagine the multi-headed creature from the 1960s Japanese movie *Ghidorah, the Three-Headed Monster*. Chris wore so many hats in the process of creating this book. He took what I wrote or said, smoothed it out, fit it together, and molded it into a story. He preserved and nurtured my voice, which let me speak directly to you. No easy feat. At the same time, he helped design everything, searched through archival photos, oversaw photo shoots, and did anything else needed to produce a book that would bring value and pleasure to our readers. This is my book, but only because Chris made it so. Domo arigato gozaimasu!

Additional thanks from Chris Ying to the following people for their help, patience, nurturing, and in-your-face physicality:

Walter Green. John Heindemause. Eli Horowitz and Russell Quinn. PFM and Dave. Kim Witherspoon. Jenny Wapner and Dawn Yanagihara and Sarah Adelman and Aaron Wehner at Ten Speed. Mom and dad and Michael and Louise and Andrew and Emma and Matthew.

And Ivan for letting me into your life, mind, restaurants, and tiny Tokyo apartment.

And of course Jami.

And Huck—I wish you could read.

A Few Words about Sourcing Ingredients

When I first began obsessing over cookbooks twenty-five years ago, I'd often find myself up against a wall when seeking out the more specialized ingredients called for in Asian recipes. I'd drive all over town to buy subpar stuff. And I lived in New York. I can only imagine and sympathize with the hair-pulling frustration of trying to make a passable bowl of mapo tofu in Iowa in 1988.

Way back when, cookbooks would list plenty of shops in Los Angeles, San Francisco, Manhattan, and Queens, and a few in Ann Arbor, Austin, and Chicago. Things are dramatically different these days. There are now small Asian grocery stores all over America. Anywhere there's a Chinese, Japanese, Korean, or Southeast Asian community, there's bound to be at least one place where you can get decent Asian ingredients.

Finally, as many other chefs have stated in many other places, the Internet is your best friend when it comes to finding ingredients. Wondering what a package of katsuobushi looks like? Consult the Goog. Need a fine-mesh strainer or a pasta roller? Ask Amazon. Can't find the flour you're looking for? Head to King Arthur Flour. Looking for a local source for fresh ramen noodles? Rip a fat Google on it.

In many cases, it costs the same to order something online as it would to buy it in the store. Plus, websites sometimes have more stock than brick-and-mortars. I tend to turn to the following sites when I can't find something locally here in New York, but there are certainly more out there.

Mitsuwa

Mitsuwa is a large chain market with outlets in Chicago, New Jersey, and California. Their website (www.mitsuwa.com) offers everything from fresh vegetables—mitsuba, Tokyo negi, nira, and daikon—to the whole spectrum of dried fish and seaweed.

Marukai

The Marukai e-store (www.marukaiestore.com) has a decent dried fish selection, as well as ramen from Sun Noodle, which is the company that is manufacturing noodles from my recipe for Ivan Ramen New York. (The Marukai site doesn't sell Ivan Ramen noodles.) The ramen comes with a broth base, which you don't have to use. The noodles are frozen fresh and make a great substitute if you're too busy to make your own noodles. Look for Sun Noodle Nama Shoyu Ramen.

H Mart

H Mart (www.hmart.com) is a massive Korean supermarket chain with locations in many states. Online, they offer a good selection of dried squid, dried sardines and anchovies, and seaweed. The actual stores are solid one-stop shops for very reasonably priced meat, fish, and vegetables.

Asian Food Grocer

Along with plush dolls and origami paper, you can order any number of Japanese food products from Asian Food Grocer (www.asianfoodgrocer.com).

About the Author and Contributors

IVAN ORKIN is a native New Yorker. He spent a total of thirteen years in Japan, but now calls Dobbs Ferry, New York home. He lives there with his wife, Mari, and three sons, but returns to Tokyo frequently.

CHRIS YING is the editor-in-chief of *Lucky Peach* and the editor and designer of the highly acclaimed *Mission Street Food* cookbook. He lives in San Francisco, California.

NORIKO YAMAGUCHI is a Tokyo-based photographer specializing in food, travel, and still-life photography. Her work has appeared in *Elle Japon* and *Bunshun*, as well as in a variety of other Japanese publications.

DANIEL KRIEGER is a New York—based food and portrait photographer. His work has appeared in numerous publications, including the *New York Times*, *Time Out New York*, and *Food & Wine*.

Index